Praise and Endorsements
for Strength in Weakness Ministries

"Guy Hammond's Strength in Weakness Ministry is helping churches address a serious void in both healing and outreach. Most Christians are not equipped to understand or converse about same-sex attraction and lifestyle, yet everyone has a friend, relative, neighbor or close member of the church for whom this is their greatest struggle. This ministry is not just for those directly hurting but for equipping all the saints. The church is fortunate that we have men like Guy who have lived at the front lines of this crucial mission. I commend him, hoping that church leaders set up a workshop to profit from Guy's gift and training."

—Steve Staten, Evangelist and Teacher; Chicago, Illinois

"I appreciate the work that Guy Hammond is pioneering in this area. He is providing an avenue by which people who have often felt forgotten or ostracized by our ministries may be understood. I appreciate Guy's willingness to teach classes that help open disciples' eyes to the needs of people within our ministries who struggle with this specific temptation."

—Dr. G. Steve Kinnard, Evangelist and Teacher; New York City, New York

"Strength in Weakness Ministries has been an answer to the prayers of many around the world who struggle with same-sex attractions, and to church leaders like myself who want to help them. This ministry is currently offering help to Christian men in India who love God but who are really troubled by their same-sex attractions. Guy's teachings and guidance have been a source of comfort, counsel and conviction for them to keep up the good fight."

Dinesh George, Evangelist; Bangalore, India

"Reaching out to those with same-sex attraction has been an area of outreach that our churches have avoided mainly due to lack of understanding and fear. Guy Hammond's honesty, humility, and loving approach are reminiscent of Jesus' outreach to all people. The Strength in Weakness Ministry is an opportunity to build bridges that have not existed before and to show true Christlike compassion to all members of our communities."

Kathleen Eastman, MSW, LSW; Chicago, Illinois

D0423588

"In this day and age when same-sex attraction has become such an emotional political issue, copious amounts of misinformation abound. Sadly, for some people the only experience with religious communities in dealing with same-sex attraction has been one of derision and malice. Guy Hammond's teaching is both biblical and personal. It is Christlike in the way it combines uncompromising conviction with unlimited compassion. The result is hope and direction for Christian and yet-to-be Christian alike. This ministry is the answer to many of our prayers. I wholeheartedly recommend Strength in Weakness to all who would like to effectively minister to those who struggle with same-sex attraction."

— *Sheridan Wright, Evangelist; New York City, New York*

"No ministry is so greatly challenged as one that attempts a truly biblical outreach to those who struggle with same-sex attraction. Either there is unseemly pandering to accommodate illicit relationships under the guise of Christian tolerance, or well-intended but naive efforts which condemn so loudly that genuine love and concern can't be heard. Walking a delicate tightrope, the Strength in Weakness ministry manages to get the balance right, presenting God's truth with humility and respect. Only one who has walked his own personal tightrope can so powerfully bring others to know the joy of obedience in the face of enormous struggle. Guy Hammond's caring and courageous ministry is a providential godsend to a segment of society that the church typically neither understands nor wishes to welcome."

— *Dr. F. LaGard Smith, Professor of law, Faulkner University, Jones School of Law; Montgomery, Alabama*

"Step-by-step instructions are great when assembling a barbeque or bicycle; however, formulaic answers are woefully inadequate when addressing questions about humanity in a fallen world. I believe both in and outside the church people are desperate for guidance and direction that does not succumb to one of the many helping models which circumvent Scripture. Strength in Weakness Ministries poignantly engages the controversial subject of homosexuality and offers wisdom, clarity and compassion—all in a culturally relevant manner."

— *Andrew Lewis, Evangelist; Toronto, Ontario, Canada*

Caring Beyond the Margins

Guy Hammond

Caring Beyond the Margins

What Every Christian Needs to Know About Homosexuality

Caring Beyond the Margins

What Every Christian Needs to Know About Homosexuality

© 2012 by Guy Hammond

Printed in the United States of America.

ISBN: 978-0-9855749-5-6

Unless otherwise indicated, all Scripture references are from the Holy Bible, New International Version, copyright 1973, 1978, 1984 by the International Bible Society. Used by permission of Zondervan Bible Publishers.

Cover and interior book design: Toney Mulhollan. The text face is set in ITC Officina Serif and Sans.

Any Internet addresses printed in this book are offered as a resource. They are not intended in any way to be or imply an endorsement by Illumination Publishers.

Illumination Publishers is committed to caring wisely for God's creation and uses recycled paper whenever possible.

Special thanks to Amy Morgan for her editorial contributions.

About the author: Guy Hammond and his wife, Cathy, were married in 1991 and have four children. In addition to his work with Strength in Weakness Ministries, he has ministered in congregations across Canada and currently works with the church in Halifax, Nova Scotia.

ILLUMINATION PUBLISHERS

www.ipibooks.com
6010 Pinecreek Ridge Court
Spring, Texas 77379-2513

Contents

Dedication

To my wife, Cathy—the miracle in my life

Acknowledgements

My wife, Cathy, and I have been on this journey together for twenty-two years. How can I thank you enough, honey, for believing in me when I often didn't believe in myself? You are the absolute love and joy of my life, the greatest gift God has ever given me. I will truly cherish you until my dying breath.

My four amazing children have been on this journey too, but they didn't have a choice—sorry about that, guys! I am aware that it's not easy for you to have a father who is same-sex attracted. Thank you for loving your dad so unconditionally and not allowing this weakness to diminish me in your eyes. You can't possibly understand how much I love you and how grateful I am to have you in my life.

My parents and my siblings are obviously such a huge part of my story. Thank you for being so patient and understanding with me as I strive to figure out this part of my life. You did not know of my same-sex-attraction issues until recently, and I want you to know that I am a faithful Christian man with an unbelievably happy and fulfilled life and that each of you is a big reason why.

My closest advisors and trusted lifelong friends, Mike and Barb Lock, Andrew and Suzette Lewis, and Sheridan and Debbie Wright, thank you for all you have done for the Hammond family.

My Advisory Board for Strength in Weakness Ministries has been so helpful. Thank you for your willingness to associate your esteemed names and reputations with this sometimes fragile and out-of-the-box ministry! Dr. Douglas Jacoby, Andrew Lewis and Dr. F. LaGard Smith, I am incredibly grateful for the kindness you have shown me.

My support staff at Strength in Weakness Ministries has helped to make my dream come true in establishing a ministry that assists same-sex-attracted Christians all over the world. None of this would have been possible without you. Thank you, Kris Boyer, Laura Jolley, Jaco Ferreira, Kathy MacBrien, Neil D'Souza, Stephen and Deb Bowen, Roy Appalsamy, Ed Bahula and Blair Frost for your continued involvement.

My fellow brothers and sisters in the Halifax-Dartmouth Church of Christ, when they first hired me, did not know all that they were getting: an evangelist, yes, but one who suffers with same-sex attractions. How can I express my immense gratitude to you for supporting my family and me and for allowing me the freedom, time and space to serve the Kingdom in this unique way? Thank you!

My friend Wendy Gritter at New Direction Ministries, thank you for teaching me the importance of "bridge-building language." I hope some day I can be as fluent and eloquent in it as you are!

Foreword

When we first met, in Canada, I had no inkling that Guy Hammond had emerged from a homosexual background. He was, to me, an affable Canadian faithfully preaching the gospel in one of the more liberal nations on our planet. Later I invited the tall Canadian to an international conference I was directing, to speak about our society's homosexual revolution. Knowing nothing of Guy's personal background—apart from the fact that he was a committed Christian—I extended the invitation only in the belief that, as a citizen of a liberal society, he would certainly prepare an interesting workshop.

Guy gave us far more than we bargained for! Opening up about his past, sharing deep feelings (both hopes and pains) with the conference participants, modeling Christian openness, and vulnerably exploring the truth in a public setting, he endeared himself to all. His workshop was a highlight of the conference. I think he also came to realize in a concrete way that he was still respected despite his background and in fact perhaps revered all the more for his courage and authenticity. Certainly my initial impression of his integrity and courage has only increased through the years.

Yet Guy Hammond's ministry has expressed itself in more than the occasional workshop on same-sex attraction. For many years now Strength in Weakness, a dynamic ministry founded by the author, has offered invaluable spiritual direction to same-sex-attracted men and women worldwide. He and his staff have also been educating church leaders and members on how to offer practical help to those with unwanted same-gender attractions, in a manner that is respectful, dignified, and compassionate.

For these reasons, it is an honor for me to commend Guy

Hammond, a trusted friend and colleague, and to recommend *Caring Beyond the Margins*. In this book you have made a wise purchase. Guy is a true pacesetter, one whom we can follow whatever lies in our personal past. May the Lord move all of us to follow his Spirit, and to live lives of genuineness, repentance, and renewal.

—Dr. Douglas Jacoby, Atlanta, Georgia
Advisory Board Member, Strength in Weakness Ministries

Introduction

My Life in the Margins

And this mess is so big
And so deep and so tall,
We cannot pick it up;
There is no way at all!

—Dr. Seuss, *The Cat in the Hat*

I used to hate being homosexually attracted; not any more. Not that I'm crazy about the idea, mind you, as this reality in my life is still somewhat of a burden to me. I certainly wouldn't argue with the Lord should the day ever arrive that he decided to zap my same-gender attractions out of me and make me a part of the heterosexual mainstream. That being said, it is true that my outlook as a Christian man who is also emotionally and physically attracted to the same sex has radically transformed since the fall of 2006. Before that time, for the first nineteen years of my Christian walk, I must say that suffering homoerotic attractions and temptations produced the same kind of chaos and disorder in my heart and mind that the Cat did in the home of two bored and unsuspecting kids in the famous children's book by Dr. Seuss, *The Cat in the Hat*. To be sure, when I looked inward, the mess that homosexuality had caused in my soul was so big and so deep and so tall that I could not pick it up and throw it away—there was no way at all! Consequently, I sadly spent almost two decades bemoaning and loathing this "thing" with which I felt I was plagued. And really, that is what it was to me: an infirmity, a disability or disease that no one, it seemed—God included—had the ability to heal.

I am not physically handicapped, and so I will not presume to understand the daily difficulties that one who is must suffer, but it is accurate to say that I spent many years believing myself to be emotionally and spiritually crippled. Indeed I felt paralyzed, confused, frustrated and most often, isolated; or shall I say, someone who lived not only outside the margins of society, but to my own detriment, the margins of the church as well. Quite frankly, in the church, living my life as a Christian while being a homosexually attracted man had for the most part been a lonely and exhausting experience.

Then, very unexpectedly, on the morning of September 19, 2006, I opened up my email inbox as I usually do to start off my day and found a message that would force me on a path of healing that I never would have believed possible. Dr. Douglas Jacoby, an internationally recognized authority in Christian apologetics, was inviting me to speak at an upcoming annual International Teachers Seminar that he was hosting in Washington D.C. My topic was "Sexual Liberation and the Gay Rights Movement." I was stunned. I had kept this information of my homosexual past and continuation of my homosexual attractions locked up tighter than Fort Knox! Except for my wife and only a few of my most trusted spiritual advisors, I spoke of this to no one. I was far too embarrassed and ashamed and fearful of rejection to let people know who I really was. So how on earth did Dr. Jacoby learn of my past? Who had betrayed my confidence and how had this private information reached his ears?

Both hurt and offended, and too terrified to broach the subject in front an audience of any kind, much less a group of international church leaders I had never met, I turned down his offer. He patiently explained that he had no prior knowledge of my issues with same-sex attractions. Then it seemed to me that the stars had aligned, that I had simply won the luck of the draw, or perhaps closer to reality, that none of the other invited speakers had wanted the controversial subject for themselves. I came to find out that Dr. Jacoby had asked no one else and simply wanted my views based on the fact that I haled from a very liberal Canada in this regard, meaning that I would have a more unique perspective on the topic than most others. Spiritually I believe that God was forcing me into having to finally address this very broken and weak area of my life that had caused so much damage and had produced an existence that was not representative of the kind of life that God had intended for me to experience. Upon coming to this realization I phoned Dr. Jacoby and accepted his invitation. I not only taught that class, but shared the story of my own homosexual past and what it was like to live with same-sex attractions as a Christian. That ninety-minute lecture and workshop was both a frightening and liberating event. It propelled me to begin this change that I have since experienced with the leading of the Holy Spirit.

How has God changed my view of this thorn in my life? What hope is there for my fellow same-sex-attracted brothers and sisters? In a nutshell (one that I will crack open further and discuss more in depth later in this book) are these four simple yet transformational truths:

1. While living a life of active homosexuality is sinful (Leviticus 18:22, 20:13; Romans 1:26–27; 1 Corinthians 6:9–10), simply being attracted to the same gender is not.

2. The primary goal for the same-sex-attracted disciple of Jesus is not to become heterosexually attracted, but to live a life of holiness while also living with same-sex attractions.

3. God is not ashamed or embarrassed of same-sex-attracted Christians. Their value and worth to him and his church are not based on that criterion.

4. Every same-sex-attracted follower of Jesus can absolutely live a successful Christian life that God would be incredibly proud of, whether or not their homoerotic appealings ever disappear.

How I Got Beyond the Margins

I began participating in homosexuality at the age of eleven, and it continued until I was twenty-four years old. By then, over a decade of acting out in homosexual activity: clandestine and anonymous sexual encounters with strangers; living a double life; hiding in plain sight; unable to be real with people I was close to, afraid I'd hurt them if they knew the truth; and a broken relationship with a boyfriend of several years had all taken their toll. Spiritually and emotionally, I knew I didn't have the strength to live like this any longer. Thankfully, God had another plan for my life.

Between the fall of 1985 and the summer of 1987 I was consistently and lovingly taught the scriptures and the biblical sexual ethic. Late in the evening on August 15, 1987 in North Toronto, Canada, both myself and the man who taught me the Bible hopped the fence of a public swimming pool long after it was closed, and just before the security guard came running out from nowhere to unceremoniously boot us out, I was baptized into Christ. I have never been involved in any kind of homosexual activity since.

What has transpired subsequent to that hot August night is a true testimony of God's astonishing power, for not only did the Lord forgive me, but he allowed me to meet and fall in love with a lovely Christian woman. Cathy and I, as of the writing of this book, have been just crazy about each other for almost twenty-two years. As if one man couldn't be blessed enough, we have been given four amazing children—two biological and two adopted—all teenagers now, and all four loved and treasured beyond their understanding. Professionally, God has seen fit to choose this very broken vessel to serve in the full-time ministry and oversee Strength in Weakness Ministries, an organization I founded that is dedicated to educating the church on the issues we are discussing in this book.

In spite of these accomplishments, as mentioned, I do continue to live beyond the margins, as the thorn of homosexual attractions is still a reality in my life even two and a half decades after leaving that existence forever. I don't understand why God works the way he does, and regardless of thousands of hours of praying and begging and confessing and reading and studying and trying, and after almost twenty-two years of marriage and raising a family and being an evangelist and leading a church, my attraction to the same gender remains. Regardless of the countless times I've asked God to take this away his answer has been: "My grace is sufficient for you, for my power is made perfect in weakness" (2 Corinthians 12:9).

Thus, I continue to live outside the lines, beyond the margins, in the fringe, for I know that because I still suffer homoerotic attractions I am considered by many, as Paul says in 1 Corinthians, one of the "lowly things of this world," one of the "despised things." I realize that in the church—because this topic is so messy and mystifying—I am still somewhat of an oddity. I understand that because I fall outside of the heterosexual mainstream my life is confusing to most, and so, beyond the margins I continue to exist. However, I don't just "exist" any longer. No,

I have in fact learned to thrive, for homosexuality used to have control over me, but by the power of God, I now have control over it.

When I began my Strength in Weakness ministry to help other same-sex-attracted disciples, I thought myself fortunate if I could connect with just thirty other fellow strugglers. Since the ministry's inception, however, I have lost count of the number of Christians from all over the world who, just like me, live with unwanted same-sex attractions. Unbeknownst to many in the church, there are numerous people in our local congregations from every continent and culture who personally battle daily with their sexual identities. In addition there are the parents and the siblings of gay children and those married to a same-sex or homosexually attracted spouse, who find themselves huddling outside the margins. They also long for credible responses in a world that is most often filled with ambiguity. And what of the church's responsibility in reaching out to the gay community?

These are daunting and intimidating issues to confront. How can the pastoral care workers who so caringly labor within our congregations: the leaders of churches, elders, deacons and small-group leaders, offer pragmatic assistance and hope for others who feel as crippled as I once did? What workable, scriptural answers can we offer to those who look to us for "good news"? These are the issues that I will address. It is my prayer that this book will be used as a reliable resource so that you will be adequately equipped to address these issues with both confidence and competence.

I confess to being somewhat of a reluctant prophet, partly because I freely admit to not having all of the answers to these very complex and multifaceted issues. I have, however, been compelled to start this ministry and to author this book so that, ultimately, Christians who are part of the heterosexual mainstream can know how to lovingly minister as Christ would to those who are not. I press on as well, for the sake of my fellow same-sex-attracted brothers and sisters and those who have family members who live with this reality, so that they can know that living outside the margin is no reason not to live victoriously as a follower of Jesus and that with Christ at the helm, this mess called homosexuality is not so big and so deep and so tall—that there is a way after all!

—Guy Hammond
Executive Director, Strength in Weakness Ministries
Halifax, Nova Scotia, Canada
June 2012

Chapter One

Homosexuality Versus Same-Sex Attraction: Which Is It?

"Nobody can go back and start a new beginning, but anyone can start today and make a new ending."

—Maria Robinson

It was a hot and humid afternoon in the summer of 1987. (Those who aren't familiar with the Canadian climate are often surprised to learn that in the summer months of July and August, temperatures can become sweltering, reaching heights of 35 to 40 degrees Celsius [95° to 104°F]). I remember it as if it were yesterday: I was sitting on bus #10 in North Toronto, Canada on my way home from a visit with my minister. Not even the punishing heat, however, is motivation enough to remember a short bus ride, as uncomfortable as it was, almost three decades later. No, my reason for such recollection is due to the decisions I made and the way the Holy Spirit moved my heart on that 20-minute trip that completely altered the direction of my life forever. I climbed aboard that bus a homosexual—a man who was hooked, a slave to my homoerotic attractions and temptations, a man unable to escape the something I felt had complete control over me—and I departed that bus, several city blocks later, never to act out homosexually again. My life had transformed for eternity.

In the previous months that I had been attending this new church, I had lived a double life: I attended church worship services and participated in all of the extracurricular events that the church hosted, but privately, much to my own shame and huge disappointment, I was powerless to stop acting out homosexually as I had been doing for many years. I continued to involve myself in a stealthy, sinful life, and the longer this continued, the worse things became.

Over time this particular minister and I had become good friends. He knew from previous discussions and times of confession what my background was. However, in an attempt to impress him and others that this kind of life and all that went with it was behind me, I had sworn to him and everyone else that my days of homosexual activity were done; but that was not true. In fact, these sinful activities had only increased, and the type of behaviors in which I had begun to participate were only more flagrant and brazen as I crossed lines that even I had said I never would. Being the wise man he was, my minister friend could sense something was "off" and feared that I had secretly continued in my homosexual life. Deciding to put an end to his suspicions, he invited me over to have a chat. When I realized what he wanted to chat about, I sat terrified and quiet.

How could I confess that I was still "gay"? How could I tell him of all of the homosexual activities I had participated in and was guilty of, especially in just the few previous months, while at the same time attending church and declaring my freedom from homosexual activity? How was I ever going to be able to verbalize in confession the filthy things I was doing? How could I explain that I was one man living two different lives: one life with these Christians and the other my secret homosexual life? How could I admit to being a coward and a hypocrite? How could I live with the rejection that was sure to come?

And then there was the harsh reality that after almost fourteen years of reliance on it, homosexuality had become a loyal and trusted friend; a mostly secret friend for sure, but a place of security and refuge that I was not too eager to abandon. Whenever I felt alone or afraid or in need of companionship, homosexuality was always willing to meet those needs. It was familiar territory to me. What of the friendships I had made in that part of my life, especially the young man with whom I had carried on a ten-year relationship? True repentance would certainly mean putting an end to our friendship forever (at least the intimate side). Was I really going to give all of that up, once and for all? Could I do it? I felt incredibly doubtful.

My minister friend was patient, kind and loving, but in spite of his best efforts to draw me out, I ultimately refused to cooperate. I had determined that the cost was too great. The most I was willing to admit was that I was indeed involved in a sinful activity that I was not going to discuss. His reply was something that stunned my heart: He simply said, "Guy, you're mocking God and his church; enough is enough. I'm going to count backwards from ten, and if you haven't started talking by the time I reach zero, if you refuse to be transparent with your life and you are not willing to repent of whatever sinful activity that you're involved in, there is nothing I can do to help you. Stop playing at Christianity and go out and fulfill your fantasies; do whatever you want, and if God lets you live through it, come back in a few years and tell me if it was worth it."

Looking back, the ten-second countdown seems a little funny now—while quite ominous at the time as he literally, slowly counted backwards from ten—but that approach certainly jolted me into finally making a choice, forcing me to stop allowing my indecision to be my decision. When the counting ended not another word was spoken. I got up and walked to the door. I looked back one last time, believing that I would never see him again. I had finally chosen to go and do whatever my heart desired. No more half in/half out. No more hypocrisy. I was fatigued from the constant conflict that was warring in my heart between "who I am" versus "what I am supposed to be."

Out to the street I went, and by the time that bus pulled up, I had planned to never go back to church again. I was tired of praying and begging that God take my homosexual attractions away. I was weary of failure. It was time to finally claim who I really was. I was done living with one foot in the church and one in the world. I confess: The idea of being set free from the constant guilt that plagued my heart while in the church was exciting.

Thoughts on how to make my escape filled my mind. How would I say good-bye to the friends I had made in the church? What would they think of me? Where would I live since living with other Christians was now going to be out of the question? I was quickly drawing up my plan to go back to my gay life and live it for all it was worth.

Apparently though, as I climbed aboard that bus, God had his own agenda for that journey home. Although I was willing to give up on him, he was not willing to give up on me. While I sat on that overcrowded bus, the Spirit kept overwhelming my mind with one thought: "Guy, Jesus died for you; you know that is a firm fact; how can you walk away from a man who allowed himself to be murdered for you?"

I knew I had it in me to quit the church and leave my friends behind. It is in my DNA to want to be alone. Left to my own accord, given a choice between being in a crowd or being by myself, the latter would win every time. Consequently, I didn't join the church because I was lonely or felt like I needed friends or because I longed to be around more people. I could have joined a local bowling league if I was in need of being a part of a group or club. I knew, therefore, that I could leave my friends and my church so that I could indulge myself in the homosexual life I was choosing; but there was no getting around a man who had died for me. No matter how hard I tried, I knew I could not deny someone who cared about me that much. I had straddled the line between Jesus who had died for me and the homosexuality that enslaved me, and I had a choice to make.

For the rest of my days I'll never forget that bus ride. By the time I had reached my stop, God had changed my heart and mind completely. Finally being put into a position where I was forced to choose between two options, once and for all, made the choice crystal clear. The dying man, Jesus, won in every scenario that I played through in my mind. I got off that bus a changed person. I knew I wanted Jesus more than I wanted the life of homosexuality. I also knew that it would not be easy and I realized that I was quite probably choosing a life of celibacy forever, but I understood the consequences of this decision. Finally a line in the sand had been drawn. Jesus was real, his death and resurrection factual, his love for me true. I believed these truths with my whole heart, and while I may have ruined everything else in my life, I decided that this one I was going to get right.

I literally stepped onto that #10 bus one man and stepped off it another. I got on that bus as a homosexual: a man who indulged in homosexuality, who cherished that secret part of his life and was willing and eager to celebrate it by how he lived and even have it trump any moral objections for the sake of personal fulfillment. I stepped off it as a man with "same-sex attractions": a man who knew he would never indulge in that activity again, who was no longer willing to keep things secret and who, through total repentance, would celebrate Jesus and the biblical sexual ethic and embrace a life of following the Lord's rules and not my own or that of our culture.

As soon as I entered my apartment, I phoned that minister, apologized, and asked if he could see me first thing the next morning. I had plenty to confess and much to repent of, and I needed his help to do it. I then went to my bedroom and read the Bible, prayed and cried for hours, asking God to give me the courage and strength to live this new life faithfully till the end. Since that day, I have never again participated in any kind of homosexual activity. It was the moment I said goodbye to that life forever, and I was baptized two weeks later. I'd be lying if I didn't tell you that it has, at times, been an incredibly difficult decision to hold to. But it's the best thing I've ever done and I wouldn't go back to that old life for anything—not *anything*.

The Difference Between "Homosexual" and "Same-Sex Attracted"

Why do I tell you that story? I want you to know the difference between homosexuality and two terms that I will use in this book many times when referring to disciples who must live with *unwanted* sexual and emotional attractions to the same gender: "same-gender attraction" and "same-sex attraction." Just as we describe the world changing forever in terms of "pre-9/11" and "post-9/11," for my life there is a very clear distinction between "pre–bus ride" and "post–bus ride" where my world changed for eternity.

The Bible makes a clear distinction between those who are active homosexuals: individuals who revel in that lifestyle and who hold no moral objections to it, versus those who, because of their understanding of Scripture, are not actively engaged in their homosexuality in a physical way and who, by their own choice and free will, refuse to compromise those convictions.

Do you not know that the wicked will not inherit the kingdom of God? Do not be deceived: Neither the sexually immoral nor idolaters nor adulterers nor male prostitutes nor homosexual offenders nor thieves nor the greedy nor drunkards nor slanderers nor swindlers will inherit the kingdom of God. And that is what some of you were. But you were washed, you were sanctified, you were justified in the name of the Lord Jesus Christ and by the Spirit of our God.

1 Corinthians 6:9–11

According to these words authored by Paul, it is the wicked who will not inherit the Kingdom of God. The apostle then goes on to explain who the wicked are. When he comes to homosexuality the Spirit saw fit to add the word "offenders." For those who were "homosexual," it was those who continue to "offend" who would be kept from the Kingdom of God. The scripture also goes on to explain that this is what some of them "were"—past tense. Their active participation in these sins—whether it was stealing, greed or homosexuality—was repented of, and they were now justified in the name of Jesus: they were washed; they were new people.

Why Is Differential Terminology Necessary?

Let me help you understand my point by asking a few questions: Is a Christian to be labeled a thief if he is tempted to steal but because of his commitment to God refuses to shoplift? No. Is a Christian to be labeled a liar if she is tempted to lie but because of her love for Jesus strives daily to tell the truth? No. Is a Christian then, to be labeled a homosexual if he or she is tempted to be sexually involved with a member of the same gender or is attracted to the same sex physically and emotionally but because of a commitment to godly purity and righteousness, refuses to give in to those temptations and commit homosexual acts? No. The answer is "no" in every single scenario because the reality is that for the disciple of Jesus, our identity is Christ; not our sexual orientation or any other defining mark. Therefore, for the disciple of Jesus who is homoerotically attracted, they are not gay or homosexual or lesbian; they are simply Christians. However, when discussing this issue, we recognize that for the point of differentiation between what is clearly sinful and what is not, some descriptive terminology is required.

Dr. Mark A. Yarhouse and Lori Burkett distinguish between the terms "same-sex attraction" and "homosexual" in their book *Sexual Identity: A Guide to Living in the Time Between the Times* in a way that I feel is extremely beneficial to this discussion:

At the *first* level, the most descriptive level, some people experience same-sex attraction. It does not necessarily mean anything more than that: it is an experience that they have, and some people experience opposite sex attractions, while others report experiencing both same- and opposite-sex attractions....Our experience is that this is the most accurate and helpful level of explanation and meaning-making for most people who experience homosexual attraction. For example, if [a man] experiences same-sex attraction, it is more accurate and more helpful for him to say of himself, "I am a man who also experiences same-sex attractions," rather than to say of himself, "I am gay." The latter suggests he is a male and that his identity rests not in his gender but in his experiences of same-sex attraction. It also suggests something about same-sex behavior being a normal expression of who he is as a person. The first way of describing himself, that is, to say, "I am a man who also experiences same-sex attraction," is merely descriptive, and it says nothing implicit about what the experiences of same-sex attraction means and what moral conclusions can be drawn from acting upon the attractions.[1]

Compare then the definition of "same-sex attraction" to those who have a "gay identity" or an identity of being a "homosexual":

[There are] those who integrate their experiences of same-sex attraction into a "gay" identity. That is, they speak of themselves with respect to a self-defining attribution, "I am gay," and this identity implicitly communicates something about how they view same-sex behavior, most often as a natural expression of who they are as a person....In contrast to the person who experiences same-sex attraction...for whom same-sex behavior is still under moral scrutiny, [he] could integrate his experiences into a "gay" identity, which carries with it the connotation that he celebrates same-sex behavior as a moral good, a natural extension of what it means to experience his sexual self-actualization in relation to himself and to others.[2]

I Am Not Gay, But I Am Same-Gender Attracted

It is for this reason that I do not consider myself to be a homosexual or gay; I do not live like a person who actively engages in homosexual relationships. I am not one who "celebrates same-sex behavior as a moral good or a natural extension of what it means to experience [my] sexual self-actualization in relation to [myself] and to others."[3] This is not my identity, and therefore I am not a homosexual. Nor do I want to use that terminology when describing myself, especially among unbelievers. It is language that will mean something to most, that I have no intention of communicating, namely that I'm still involved in active homosexual behavior, which I am not.

I do, however, live with unwanted same-gender attractions, though I have committed myself to not entertaining those appetites. I have *chosen* to walk along another path as I strive to follow Jesus. This is a decision that I make every day. Colossians 4:5–6 tells us, "Be wise in the way you act toward outsiders; make the most of every opportunity. Let your conversation be always full of grace, seasoned with salt, so that you may know how to answer everyone." So the words we use matter.

A Beautiful Mind

In 2001 in a movie called *A Beautiful Mind*, Russell Crowe portrayed the Hollywood version of the real life of American mathematician and Nobel Prize winner in Economic Sciences, John Forbes Nash Jr. As a young man, John Nash Jr. was diagnosed with paranoid schizophrenia and spent periods of time in psychiatric hospitals due to the delusions that he often suffered. Near the end of the movie portrayal, John Nash is asked if the visions have left him. I love the reply, for while I cannot personally relate to the challenges of mental illness, the response certainly does reflect the battle I fight in regard to my same-sex attractions. If I were asked the question, "Are your homosexual attractions gone?" I would come close to the same response that we hear in the movie:

No, they're not gone. And maybe they never will be. But I've gotten used to ignoring them, and I think as a result, they've kind of given up on me. You think that's what it's like with all our dreams and our nightmares? You've gotta keep feeding them for them to stay alive?[4]

Likewise, my homosexual attractions are not gone, and maybe they never will be, but I have gotten used to ignoring them. As a result, I have experienced huge amounts of victory over them—and they have largely given up on me. I simply have decided that I am not going to feed these appetites, making it difficult for them to stay alive.

In the final scene of the movie interpretation, John Nash gives his acceptance speech for the Nobel Prize. Here he says,

> I've always believed in numbers, in the equations and logics that lead to reason....But after a lifetime of such pursuits I ask: What truly is logic? Who decides reason? My quest has taken me to the physical, the metaphysical, the delusional, and back. And I have made the most important discovery of my career, the most important discovery of my life: It is only in the mysterious equations of love that any logical reasons can be found.[5]

Similarly, in my life, my quest for fulfillment, peace and happiness has taken me to many places, but by traveling this journey I have made the most important discovery of my life: It is only in the mysterious and spiritual equations of Christian love, obedience and faith that any true and long-lasting fulfillment of the soul can ever be discovered.

So while some may want to identify those of us who come from a homosexual past or who still live with unwanted same-gender attractions and label us "gay" or otherwise, to God we are simply his children (John 1: 11–13, Romans 8:16–17). Christians are not gay, or lesbian, or homosexual. There is so much more to their lives than their sexual orientations. They are as Alan Chambers says:

> Great husbands and wives, loving parents, loyal and trustworthy friends, sons and daughters, brothers and sisters, trusted employees and helpful contributors to our communities and churches, but first and foremost they are Christians: loved sons and daughters of God.[6]

The Freedom of Choice

"OK, Guy, congratulations, you haven't acted out in any kind of homosexual activity since that bus ride home about thirty years ago. Great. But how do you remedy still being attracted to other men while also being a Christian? After all, God calls homosexuality 'detestable' (Leviticus 18:22, 20:13) and I just can't imagine a follower of Jesus actually being tempted to lust after other men." Well, let me put it this way: I was not able to instantly change my sexual orientation at baptism any more than a heterosexual is able to change his or her unwanted temptations at baptism.

Not that I wouldn't have loved that happening. If I had a dollar for every time I begged God to zap me into a heterosexually attracted man, I'd be living in a villa in the south of France and I would have gotten there in my private jet. I would love to tell you that I got out of the waters of baptism on August 15, 1987 and everything just changed. But it didn't. What did change was: 1) the forgiveness I now had from acting out homosexually, and 2) the Spirit of God living inside me—which now gives me the strength and power to deny myself every day in order to be righteous and obedient. God didn't take away the temptations but rather has given me something even better than the elimination of homosexual temptation: the ability to deny those enticements and to choose God in their place.

That is real freedom: the ability to choose. I may not ever have chosen my sexual orientation (and I did not choose it, but more on that later), but I sure do have the capability to select what I am going to do with my mind and my physical body and can unequivocally choose what I will cherish in my heart. I consider this to be one of the most amazing features of Christianity, and one that is often overlooked: the ability for one to actually choose how they will live their lives. The follower of Jesus does not have to be a victim to every thought and temptation, or to what society determines to be appropriate and acceptable.

Before I found Christ, I was a slave, unable to turn away from homosexuality, mostly because there was no other viable alternative that was being offered. Frustration with my inability to refuse something I knew deep down was morally wrong and ultimately unfulfilling led me searching for explainable reasons as to why I continued down that path. The most reasonable answer and the one that I believed gave me control and power in the place of choice was that I "had to be me"; that somehow I would be betraying who I really was if I did not embrace my homosexuality. The truth is that I couldn't help being that person. Even though I knew that what I was doing was wrong, I simply did not have the capability to stop. I was being "me" not because I was choosing it freely, but because there simply were no other viable choices available. In this sense I did not choose homosexuality; homosexuality chose me. How frustratingly hopeless things seemed to me then! By deciding to follow Jesus, however, I actually was presented with a choice between two clearly distinct alternatives: homosexuality and Christianity.

Speaking to the matter of choice, Dr. Mark A. Yarhouse and Lori Burkett say that

> Sexual orientation refers to the direction of a person's attractions. Scientists and researchers propose a number of theories about what causes a person to experience same-sex attraction or to have a homosexual orientation. The bottom line is that scientists do not really know for certain why one person experiences same-sex attraction and another does not....We are suggesting that people have little say over whether they experience same-sex attractions to begin with. If you are experiencing same-sex attractions or believe you have a homosexual orientation, we believe it is not something you did or failed to do that led you to have these attractions. However, it is clear that a person can choose to act or refrain from acting on their attractions.[7]

The ability to actually choose from the variety of options presented to us brings liberation and independence. Lack of choice and being forced into any one way of life or thought because there simply is no other route made available is what we call socialism or communism in the political theatre. In the spiritual realm, however, it is just simply called hopelessness.

I've heard many same-sex-attracted individuals argue what I used to say to myself: "I must be true to myself. I am who I am—a homosexual." For the Christian who is same-gender attracted, such an argument loses all steam when we admit that who we really are is Christians. That reality trumps everything, including sexual orientation! Christianity is our nature and we can't truly be at peace and true to ourselves unless we are following God's path for our lives.

As stated, just because I have been blessed with the freedom to choose what I will allow my mind to dwell on and am now capable of determining my actions because of the alternative that Jesus provides, does not mean that my homoerotic feelings, emotions, attractions and temptations have abandoned me. What are we to make of this?

What Does "Struggle" Mean?

I don't always like using the word "struggle" when describing what it's like to live as a Christian who is same-sex attracted. For those of us of this persuasion, it is a struggle in the sense that we must contend with this component of our lives that is so unwelcome, but beyond this, to say that we "struggle" with homosexuality somehow puts the same-sex attracted disciple at a disadvantage compared to the majority of the heterosexual mainstream because of the inferences that are often assumed when employing this word.

What opposite-sex-attracted follower of Jesus would ever say, "I 'struggle' with heterosexuality"? No one. The term "heterosexual" is merely descriptive of sexual preference, not a commentary on the severity or frequency of the stimuli that is experienced or whether or not the person is sexually active. In other words, the word is neutral. The attraction to the opposite sex is not always in motion. Except for a very minute minority of the population who clearly suffer attractions beyond what would be considered a healthy norm, almost all heterosexually attracted individuals experience only periodic attractions to the opposite sex; they do not live in a constant state of heightened attraction, experiencing sexual arousal toward every member of the opposite gender. Even though subconsciously the attractions are automatic and involuntary, in order for erotic stimuli to cause arousal, certain criteria must first be met. These criteria are based on any number of factors: race, body type, age, facial features, weight, height and personality, to name just a few. If these conditions are not met, no "attraction" will be experienced.

The same is true for same-sex-attracted individuals. As a homosexually attracted man, I do not live in a constant state of erotic arousal when in the company of other men. Yet I've had people tell me that it has been their assumption that the same-sex-attracted person experiences desirability toward every member of the same gender; in other words, the attraction is always in motion; we are always "struggling." This erroneous notion unfairly takes the neutrality out of any term that can be used to describe those who suffer homoerotic capabilities.

Sadly, when this occurs, same-gender-attracted Christians are not given the same credit as heterosexually attracted individuals. I can tell you plainly that I am not physically attracted to most members of my own gender, and those men who have feared that they need to keep their distance because surely I must be attracted to them are thinking way too highly of themselves! Like any heterosexually attracted individual, even though the attractions are automatic and involuntary, they will not be awakened unless certain criteria are met in my subconscious; and they too are based on any number of numerous factors. If those criteria are not met, no attraction is ever experienced.

As a homosexually attracted follower of Jesus, I do not "white-knuckle" my way through life. I do not live in a constant state of "struggle." Certainly, I have my moments when I face temptation in this regard, but for the most part, these episodes are fleeting and periodic, and when they are experienced, I must do what every other Christian in the world must do when Satan comes calling: I must pray and act quickly to conquer that temptation, and for the times that I fail, I must immediately turn to God for his mercy and healing.

What Causes Attraction?

In an interview I had with him as I prepared for this project, Dr. Mike Rosebush, an internationally distinguished professional counselor and former vice president of Focus On the Family, who has had years of experience helping literally hundreds of males overcome pornography, sexual addiction, and homosexuality, provided the following analogy to sexual attraction:

Why is it that one person would be drawn to a red Corvette while another is drawn to a mid-1970s grey Russian Lada? (OK, so I can't imagine that one either, but you get my point.) Why is it that one could be walking down a busy street and see a thousand cars within his peripheral sight and not have one stand out to him. Then his eyes quickly glance over that red Corvette; that particular vehicle suddenly stands out from among all the other cars on the road as the one vehicle that meets his criteria of what is an amazing car, and suddenly his neck is craning, his eyes are zeroing in, and he's just got to get a closer look at that specific vehicle.

Is it sinful that he is attracted to that particular type of car? No, it's just an attraction at this point. There is neither good nor bad; it just is. But let's say that this individual starts to constantly dream about owning a red Corvette, becomes jealous of everyone else who can afford one and starts planning a way to steal one. Or let's suppose he becomes so obsessed with owning one that it develops into an all-encompassing fixation? That is when he obviously would have crossed the line of simply having an attraction for that car to now sinning in his desire to get that car, the car consuming his thoughts and affecting his behavior.

Why is it that heterosexual men prefer women with large breasts and a low waist-to-hip ratio, which are seen as signs of fertility; and heterosexual women like men with muscular shoulders and a broad chest, which are signs of strength and protection; while the homosexually oriented find those very same features in the opposite gender unappealing? Science has yet to completely unlock the secrets of what causes us to be attracted to someone or something, and quite frankly, the Bible does not address this either. My main point in this chapter is not to discuss causation but rather to point out that the initial attraction to the same gender is not sinful; a departure from God's initial plan for our lives, yes; sinful, no. What God is most concerned about is not to what we are attracted, but what we do with those attractions and the temptations we face because of them.

As stated, just because I have been blessed with the freedom to choose what I will allow my mind to dwell on and am now capable of determining my actions because of the alternative that Jesus provides, does not mean that my homoerotic feelings, emotions, attractions and temptations have abandoned me. What are we to make of this?

There is a truth that every disciple needs to recognize and truly acknowledge regarding this issue, especially if they have any desire to offer credible assistance to homosexuals who look to the church for help and guidance, and to the same-gender-attracted Christian who needs constant support and encouragement: Being attracted to the same sex is not a sin. Period. Just being attracted to something is not sinful.

The orientation of being "same-gender attracted" is, in and of itself, neither good nor bad; it just is. It is not a sin that I am same-sex attracted any more than it is a sin that someone else is opposite-sex attracted. Left alone, these terms are neutral.

"Contrary to Nature" in Romans 1:26–27

That being said, I certainly understand and agree with the apostle Paul's declaration in Romans 1: 26–27 where he pronounces that homosexuality is contrary to nature: "For this reason God gave them up to dishonorable passions. For their women exchanged natural relations for those that are contrary to nature" (ESV). Robert A. Gagnon writes,

> Given the meaning of "contrary to nature" (*para physin*) and comparable expressions used by Jewish writers of the period to describe same-sex intercourse, the meaning of the phrase by Paul is clear: minimally, Paul is referring to the anatomical and procreative complementarity of male and female.[8]

I will add here that it was not God's intention that I experience homoerotic appetites even though I do not involve myself in homosexual activity. In this sense, homosexual attraction is not natural, but this does not mean it is sinful. In this fallen and broken world, do we not all at times experience desires, inclinations, leanings or appetites that are not representative of what God initially intended for our lives, meaning that they are unnatural?

It is natural to desire food; it is not, however, God's will that we desire it so powerfully that we risk our health in consuming it. Many Christians live with the desire to self-medicate through overindulgence in alcohol. Is the temptation to do so, by itself, sinful? No. It certainly is not what God intended, and in this sense it is unnatural, but it is not sinful to experience this desire. In the same fashion, the disciple who has a sexual bias or predisposition toward the same gender is not in sin because he or she experiences this specific appetite. It certainly is unnatural in the sense that it is not representative of what the Lord initially intended, but that does not make it sin.

Hebrews 4:15 says that "we do not have a high priest who is unable to sympathize with our weaknesses, but we have one who has been tempted in every way, just as we are—yet was without sin." So Christ experienced sexual temptation, meaning that there were times when he really wanted to sin sexually, and based on Hebrews 4:15, it could be effortlessly surmised that Christ certainly experienced homoerotic temptations as well, but he consistently stayed pure and righteous. Did Jesus ever sin by experiencing heterosexual or homosexual temptations? Clearly not.

Experiencing a homoerotic temptation is not sinful, just as experiencing same-sex attractions are not. Both automatically occur and are involuntary. The key issue is what we *do* with the temptation that makes our actions either sinful or holy.

Why Facing Temptation Is a Thrilling Moment in Time

How can any disciple of Christ judge or punish anyone for undergoing any kind of attraction or temptation? The truth about temptation is this: The lure to sin is as much an occasion for you and me to do the right thing as it is for us to do the wrong thing. God allows temptation in order to develop our spiritual life (James 1:2–3). Temptation provides the opportunity for each of us to choose between what is right and what is wrong. Every time we overcome and defeat temptation, regardless of what form it arrives in, we become more like Jesus! There are few things we will do in life to become more like Christ than to say "no" to sinful enticements. Temptation is a pivotal instant in time when the follower of Jesus will stand alone and have the alternative to do right or to do wrong based solely on their own choice. It is a key instant in time when God and his angels will stop to see whether the Christian will just "talk" about being a follower of Jesus, or will actually "walk" like Jesus. There will rarely be a more thrilling part in the disciple's day than when they're tempted and have this chance to declare to the universe to whom they will be truly devoted. Shall we then use that glorious opportunity to honor God as an opportunity to judge, look down on and even ridicule simply because the appetite that gives birth to that temptation is atypical or considered to be offensive?

One of the mantras of Strength in Weakness Ministries, to which I believe Christians who live with unwanted same-sex attractions must cling, is a statement that did not originate with me, but one that I often repeat: "The goal is not heterosexuality, it is holiness." As is the case with every other sin in every other area of life, when we do sin, we trust that God's grace is sufficient. We will be making tremendous strides in the church if we can all recognize and live as though same-gender-attracted disciples and their weaknesses are not bad public relations for the Kingdom and for God, but rather vessels for the Lord's use.

Let Jesus' church, then, never deserve to be accused of being ashamed or embarrassed of those in the battle with homoerotic attractions, but rather let it provide a home of safety and security, a haven where the majority of those who live within the margins of heterosexual attraction appreciate and value those who do not. For I can tell you confidently that the same-sex-attracted disciples in your local congregation have had to experience their own metaphoric "bus ride home": a time when they had to courageously decide once and for all what they would embrace for the rest of their lives, homosexuality or Jesus who was willing to die for them. For those of us who have stayed faithful, the dying man has won every time, and each of us has determined that while we may not be able to go back and start a new beginning, we will live each and every day in such a manner as to make a new ending.

Resources

1. Joe Dallas and Nancy Heche, *The Complete Guide to Understanding Homosexuality* (Eugene, OR: Harvest House, 2011).
2. Alan Chambers, *God's Grace and the Homosexual Next Door* (Eugene, OR: Harvest House, 2006).

Chapter One Endnotes

1. Mark A. Yarhouse and Lori A. Burkett, *Sexual Identity: A Guide to Living in the Time Between the Times* (New York: University Press of America, 2003), 30.

2. Ibid., 30–31.

3. Ibid.

4. *A Beautiful Mind*, directed by Ron Howard (Hollywood, CA: Universal Studios, 2001).

5. Ibid.

6. Alan Chambers, "Hope for Those Who Struggle" lecture, Exodus International Conference, Concordia University, Irvine, CA, July 26, 2007.

7. Yarhouse and Burkett, 5–6.

8. Robert A. J. Gagnon, *The Bible and Homosexual Practice: Texts and Hermeneutics* (Nashville, TN: Abingdon Press, 2001), 254.

Chapter Two

How Homosexuality Deceived Me

You can learn to love anything.
Even a bird in a cage will sing a song.
Even if it kills you in the end;
Pick your poison.

—George Strait, country music singer

I was raped by a man when I was eight years old. It is the first memorable event in my life that I'm confident contributed to my sexual identity confusion. To what extent, I'll never be able to say with full accuracy, but to be sure, it did very clearly serve as one of the underpinnings for how I viewed relationships with other males for years to come. Of course, study after study has shown that childhood sexual abuse almost always results in long-term psychological, emotional and physical damage and can cause long-term problems including difficulty in relationships, substance abuse, loss of education and even income-earning potential. Being that I find it arduous to hold a simple conversation with even an acquaintance for more than a moment or two without wanting to hyperventilate, much less build a lasting friendship; have struggled significantly with my weight for most of my life and most certainly have an addictive personality; and have done extremely poorly in school including failing a grade, I suppose in my experience, one could make the argument that those findings would be true to some extent. I'll also add that Christ's teachings on love, coupled with a determination to not allow myself to be a complete recluse means that yes, I do actively engage in conversation with strangers and friends alike; so don't worry, I am not a hermit. I also do make the occasional trip to the gym, attempt to not gorge too much on Ben and Jerry's, have done a decent job in educating myself, and am transparent with my addictive tendencies; I am able to stay out of trouble.

However, I do find it interesting how I can look back in adulthood and see these pieces connect. Whatever the case, this I can say with full accuracy: Suffering childhood sexual abuse by a man was one of the many ingredients in the recipe that made me who I am today in regard to my sexual identity confusion. Certainly, those events in my youth were utterly confusing to me, and I did not ever speak of it to anyone—including my wife—until I was in my late thirties.

Why Homosexuality Was So Alluring

I grew up going to church. With my dad as the minister and my mom playing the role of the traditional minister's wife, I mostly remember feeling safe and happy in my home environment as a child. Somewhere in my preteen years, however, my folks experienced great difficulties in their relationship, and things between them took a toll on the atmosphere at home. In spite of "who we were" on Sundays when we went to church, things were pretty screwed up behind the scenes; no one knew about it but the three of us. I won't get into details on who did what, because I love my parents, they have apologized, and I have forgiven them. Now that I am the father of four teenagers myself, I do look back with much more compassion for what they must have been going through. Also, should the day ever come that one of my four kids feels the need to share about some of my most regrettable moments as a father (God help me), I hope that they would do so delicately and with kindness. So let me just say this: By the time I was eleven or twelve years old (right at the time that I was first introduced to homosexuality), the problems at home were in full swing.

My father was also ill most of the time, so spending time at home had become an undesirable option. By this stage in his life, my dad was distant and too enveloped in his own problems to do much with me. In my early preteen and teen years I felt abandoned. It would not be far from the truth to say that I had no real example to follow on how to properly behave as a boy or young man during these incredibly formative years. My grades in school plummeted; as mentioned earlier, I was forced to repeat a grade in school. I also chose a group of guys to hang out with who were definitely the wrong crowd, and that's where I started making some really bad choices for my life.

My First Time

It was also during this period of time that a kid I went to school with asked me if I wanted to play a new game he had learned (from whom I have no idea) that involved us playing cards where the loser took off his clothes. Having grown up in an extremely conservative Christian home, I wasn't sure what sin was worse: playing cards (that almost guaranteed that the hand of God would reach down from heaven and hurl me into the depths of a fiery hell) or taking off my clothes with some kid in my bedroom.

While the hand of God may not have struck me down, a whole new world of sin and dissoluteness that was now open to me certainly did. Needless to say, things went downhill pretty quickly, and this kid and I carried on a sinful relationship with each other into our early twenties. From our mid-teens on we considered ourselves to be "boyfriends." What I found in this relationship—and with the others I was involved with on the side during this time—was the acceptance, attention and love that I craved but could not find at home. While I knew that what I was doing was wrong, emotionally I was starving, and so I kept going back. People who are emotionally starved will do anything to get those very real emotional needs met, whatever the cost. It is a true statement that "bad love is better than no love at all."

Years of Confusion

Between the ages of twelve and fifteen especially, I remember how confusing it all seemed. I knew that I was different from those around me because when puberty hit, my attraction was toward boys, while all of my friends were now interested in girls. Of course, as with everyone in this age bracket, the opinions of my friends was critical to me, so when they so eagerly threw out jokes about gays, queers, homos, perverts, freaks and fags when referring to homosexuals, another piece of me would die inside, knowing that I was one of these people that everyone else thought so little of. A whole new world of shame entered my heart that I had never experienced before.

When I was alone, I'd think about how little the world seemed to think of me, and I took it personally as it stuck like a knife in my chest. The loneliness of being an outcast was overwhelming.

At home, whenever the subject of homosexuality came up, I remember my father eagerly displaying his disgust of these people and how wicked and evil and repugnant they were, as I weakly approved, knowing that I was one of those people whom my own father and all of my friends hated.

Homosexuality and God

As I grew in my teen years, I appeared to everyone else to be a great Christian kid. I was involved as much as possible at church and at the Christian high school I attended. I prayed every day that God would forgive me and change me. I kept going to church; I got baptized—twice—thinking that what I was doing was so evil that one baptism couldn't possibly be enough to cleanse me of this sin in my life.

I did all I could do to be popular; I was funny, accepted and loved—everything that I didn't feel on the inside. In my attempt to be "normal" and like everyone else, I had a few girlfriends in high school, which felt awkward, strange and completely unnatural. Meanwhile, I secretly carried on my sexual relationship with my boyfriend.

From the ages of nineteen to twenty-one I volunteered on a missionary team in Papua New Guinea where I climbed through the jungles and taught people the Bible, worked in a hospital, ran a first-aid clinic—you know, the regular missionary stuff. Those were two amazing years: two years and no homosexual contact with anyone. I had been hoping that this reprieve would heal me, but it was short-lived, as not long after returning home, I was back to my old ways, and soon I was crossing lines that I had said I never would. I was confident that no one could possibly love me if they knew who I really was.

As far as church is concerned, I can certainly relate to the unique paradox that this author describes: "It's one thing to struggle, but another to feel you're the only one struggling. Worse yet is the fear that if your problem were found out, the grace shown to people with 'normal' problems wouldn't be extended to you."[1] This was a very lonely way to live. I felt like an alien in this heterosexual world: I was different from my friends—both in the church and out.

Whenever homosexuality was talked about from the pulpit, it was the epitome of what the church was against; it was preached that it was evil, disgusting and deplorable, that it was an abomination before God, deserving of death. I therefore lived really believing that *I* must be evil, disgusting, deplorable and an abomination before God. I believed I deserved to die and burn in hell and my entire life was a joke to be laughed about. Not a very good recipe for building a healthy self-esteem.

I seriously doubted God's love for me. I knew that I couldn't possibly be spiritually saved with this thing in my life. I was terrified of going to hell, so at night while falling asleep I would pray, beg, plead, cry and shout to God imploring that I would wake up the next morning and be different, straight, hetero, normal—anything but what I was; and this was my ritual for years.

Not long after my return from Papua New Guinea I became firmly convinced that this was how I was born, certain that change was not possible and confident that God had no intention of making me "normal." I felt quite deserted by God, frankly, and extremely confused as to why this "loving" God would allow me to suffer with such a difficult problem in my life—a problem that I had no ability to change or conquer on my own. It was this thing that on the one hand I loved, but it was a thing that I also hated. I spent the next couple of years indifferent to God and moral limits, so I jumped right into the homosexual lifestyle, all the while keeping up the hypocritical façade of church attendance and the routine of living in what felt like two separate worlds. However, since homosexuality was the only "fix" I had known for so many years, it only made sense to me to continue going to what was familiar and what would make me feel better.

The truth was that not only was my life broken, but my heart was too. The more I indulged myself in the things that were feeding that emotional need, the more frustrated I felt with myself. The deep chasm in my heart was expanding at a rate I couldn't fill, and there is no doubt that for a while homosexuality quenched the legitimate emotional deficiencies in my life. But the relief was only momentary and I was left feeling emptier and emptier as time went on.

Looking for the Real Thing

Many desire true intimacy with God but instead will settle for rules and rituals, an imitation that bring no closeness with the Creator at all. And here is the ingeniousness, the cleverness of the lie of homosexuality. The enemy loves to imitate God, "for Satan himself masquerades as an angel of light" 2 Corinthians 11:14. Satan pretends to be something that he is not and tries to sell us goods and products that promise abundance but that eventually deliver spiritual and emotional merchandise never advertised. He takes something that is evil and that will ultimately poison us spiritually and makes it appear satisfying, pleasing and fulfilling—for the moment. This is how Satan plays mind games with humanity; and there are few groups of people with whom he has been more successful in his cunning deceit than those like me, who have fallen for the lie of homosexuality. It promises so much and delivers so desperately little. It is truly one of the greatest rip-offs that Satan has ever perpetrated on mankind. Of course, we see this at play everywhere. Homosexuals are hardly the only ones who have been duped.

Many long for the intimacy and commitment of a lifelong covenant partner but end up settling for a cheap imitation of living together outside of marriage. It is not the real thing. The truth is that all of us are guilty of going to the wrong place to quench our emotional thirsts, only to discover that while the activity helped for a time, it was just a momentary satisfaction of our deepest craving.

To illustrate my point, I will turn to a consumer product we can all relate to: a can or bottle of non-diet soda. Who doesn't love an ice-cold Coke on a hot, sunny day? It is the leading cola brand for a reason—but as good as it tastes, there are some side effects that most of us rarely consider while drinking it. A study was done in 2006 to determine what drinking one can of Coke will do to the body within sixty minutes of consumption. This study, by the way, pointed out that Coke is not the only culprit, but that the process and effects on the body are the same for any non-diet soda. In short, says the study: "It wreaks havoc on the human organism." And the main reason is sugar:

- In the first 10 minutes: 10 teaspoons of sugar hit your system. (100% of your recommended daily intake.) You don't immediately vomit from the overwhelming sweetness because phosphoric acid cuts the flavor, allowing you to keep it down.

- 20 minutes: Your blood sugar spikes, causing an insulin burst. Your liver responds to this by turning any sugar it can get its hands on into fat....

- 40 minutes: Caffeine absorption is complete. Your pupils dilate; your blood pressure rises; as a response your liver dumps *more sugar* into your bloodstream. The adenosine receptors in your brain are now blocked, preventing drowsiness.

- 45 minutes: Your body ups your dopamine production, stimulating the pleasure centers of your brain. This is physically the same way heroin works, by the way.

- 60 minutes: The phosphoric acid binds calcium, magnesium and zinc in your lower intestine, providing a further boost in metabolism. This is compounded by high doses of sugar...increasing the urinary excretion of calcium.

- 60 minutes: The caffeine's diuretic properties come into play (It makes you have to [urinate]). It is now assured that you'll evacuate the bonded calcium, magnesium, and zinc that were headed to your bones as well as sodium, electrolytes, and water.

- 60 minutes: As the rave inside of you dies down, you'll start to have a sugar crash. You may become irritable and/or sluggish. You've also now, literally, [urinated] away all the water that was in the Coke. But not before infusing it with valuable nutrients your body could have used for things like hydrating your system, or build strong bones and teeth.[2]

Maybe we should pause here for a moment to allow those of us who have soft drinks in our refrigerators to pour them down the sink! Not to mention the fact that the study was centered on a regular 591-ml bottle and not the super-sized, mega-thirst-quenching kind (three times the volume—yes, that's thirty teaspoons of sugar!) that we get at most movie theatres, convenience stores or at a fast-food restaurant when we upsize our order.

Considering the above information, it's almost revolting to think about the amount of abuse our internal systems are suffering, all while we sit comfortably in our full-cushioned, high-backed, reclining chairs—each one providing its own personal cup holder large enough for a container the size of a bucket—while we watch our favorite film.

The really fascinating thing is that even though we know that these drinks are incredibly unhealthy, most of us still drink them! In fact, I'm sure it's a very safe bet that even though you have now been equipped with the findings of this study, sometime in the near future you'll most likely have another Coke and put your body into shock again. Why? Because on a hot sunny day, or while watching something blow up on a gigantic screen, there are few things that taste better than an ice-cold Coke. After all, "It's the real thing"—right? Wrong. I think next time I go to a movie, I'll just ask for water!

Yet We Drink the Stuff Anyway!

While the disturbing details listed above will most likely cause you to think twice the next time you reach for a soft drink, the truth is that we have in fact always known that drinking a bottle of soda is bad for you. You didn't need a study to tell you that. You're well aware that this stuff is just a mixture of sugar, coloring and chemicals such as phosphoric acid, which by the way, is also tremendous for the removal of rust from the bumper of your car. (Of course, to help us feel better about what we're throwing down our gullet, there are the sodas that advertise that their mixture is laced with "natural flavor." Mmmmm..., now doesn't that sound good?) You see, even though colas aren't good for us, they still quench our thirst. They still meet the need, even if it is only momentarily.

The same is true for homosexuality. This is why it is so alluring to some: because for those who are same-gender attracted, it quenches our thirst—our genuine emotional thirst—even if only momentarily. As the country superstar George Straight so correctly sings, "You can learn to love anything. Even a bird in a cage will sing a song. Even if it kills you in the end; pick your poison."[3]

It's Not about the Sex

At its core, homosexuality is a relational problem, not a sexual problem. That's right, I said it—it's not about the sex—and herein lies a significant truth about homoerotic attraction. Homosexuality in fact has very little to do with sex. Every person who struggles with homosexuality is really just striving to have some very legitimate emotional and relational needs met in a very illegitimate manner. It is crucial for you to know from the outset that as long as you believe that homosexuality is primarily a sexual issue, you'll be unable to adequately assist someone who is striving to overcome their homoerotic impulses, and with them the very real, underlying and genuine emotional deficiencies that are causing the problem.

As already stated, this is true of all types of unhealthy or even sinful actions. Jesus, being the architect of the heart, was and is able to see beyond the surface, to look much deeper than everyone else and zero in on the real problem.

For instance, let's take the story of the woman that Jesus met at the well in John chapter 4:

> Jesus replied, "Anyone who drinks this water will soon become thirsty again. But those who drink the water I give will never be thirsty again. It becomes a fresh, bubbling spring within them, giving them eternal life."
>
> "Please, sir," the woman said, "give me this water! Then I'll never be thirsty again, and I won't have to come here to get water."
>
> "Go and get your husband," Jesus told her.
>
> "I don't have a husband," the woman replied.
>
> Jesus said, "You're right! You don't have a husband—for you have had five husbands, and you aren't even married to the man you're living with now. You certainly spoke the truth!"
>
> John 4:13–18 NLT

This is a story about a lonely and troubled soul who was trying desperately to quench a spiritual and emotional thirst. There was no permanent satisfaction in the multiple relationships she had experienced. In fact, each time a relationship ended, she needed to go and find a new mate, hoping that this next man would fulfill all of her emotional desires. Time and time again, however, she was left sadly disappointed, and this is the reason that by the time she encountered Jesus she was into her sixth relationship. Jesus told her that she would never find the fulfillment she so desperately longed for by going to this same old well as she had been doing for years. Only he had the answer; only he had the clean, pure water that would quench these thirsts and heal the brokenness forever.[4]

The Big Rip-Off

My life mirrors that woman's in many ways. Before giving my life over to Jesus, there were few things that I turned to more than homosexuality in order to quench my emotional thirsts. From my youth, with all of those problems in my home life and all of the fears and insecurities in my own heart, whenever I felt lonely, afraid, unloved, insignificant or unconfident, I learned to turn to homosexuality to meet those very real needs. And it worked. Participating in those relationships and activities *did* leave me feeling satisfied, loved, cared for, accepted and important. After a short time, however (like the woman at the well), I was always left feeling even thirstier, more empty and alone, thereby forcing me to involve myself even further in these relationships and activities to quench the emotional thirst yet again. It was a never-ending cycle, but I just didn't realize it.

The sad truth is that I spent a lot on homosexuality, a lot of time and energy just wasted: hours, days, and months, even years that I will never get back. I spent a lot of money too, all to drink something that would never satisfy me to begin with.

God, through the prophet Isaiah, begs each of us see reason:

"Come, all you who are thirsty,
   come to the waters;
and you who have no money,
   come, buy and eat!
Come, buy wine and milk
   without money and without cost.
Why spend money on what is not bread,
   and your labor on what does not satisfy?

Listen, listen to me, and eat what is good,
 and your soul will delight in the richest of fare.
Give ear and come to me;
 hear me, that your soul may live.
I will make an everlasting covenant with you,
 my faithful love promised to David."

Isaiah 55:1–3

Are we not all the same? Has not each one of us, regardless of our sexual orientation or area of brokenness and temptation gone to the wrong well to drink, only to be left thirstier than when we began?

Do you and I not deserve better? God thinks so. He calls out to you and me and begs us to come to him—that our souls may live. What God offers is free. It will cost us nothing, and it is the only thing that will quench our hurts, fears and insecurities.

I know now that homosexuality will never, ever give me what I really need or even want, but it will always (100% of the time) leave me emotionally and spiritually thirsty. Only when I decide to satisfy my thirst with the living water that Jesus offers me will I ever be truly satisfied.

When Jesus entered my life and offered me something that was so much more quenching and satisfying than anything homosexuality could ever provide, and when I came to my senses and realized that he was offering me water—a living water that would gratify my emotional needs in a lasting and eternal way that homosexuality never possibly could—Jesus became the obvious choice, the real thing, the better well to draw my water from; it is there that I gladly drink from today.

For every Christian, there was a time when every one of us went with what we knew, with what we had learned, with what worked, given our limited options. Even though most of the time we knew that these things were hurting us, we still participated in them because they worked; they quenched our thirsts, if only for a little while.

We've all spent years drinking in something that satisfied our thirsts for only a short amount of time. Every single one of us is guilty of buying these counterfeit goods. Whether our issue was with alcohol, drugs, relationships, overeating, bulimia, sexual addictions, pornography, addictions to work, sleep, Internet shopping, gambling, smoking, video games, online games or homosexuality, are we not all the same?

The Whisperings of Satan

It's been my experience that Satan has tried to capitalize on these weaknesses in my life. I can't tell you how many times I have thought to myself, "I'm a loser." At least that is what Satan so often has whispered or rather, hissed, into my inner ear. There's another name for same-sex-attracted losers like me; they're called "Wemmicks." Back in the mid-1990s Max Lucado authored a series of children's books. His first was entitled *"You Are Special."* It's one of my very favorite books because I can so relate to its main character, Punchinello. In the story we're told of small wooden people called "Wemmicks."

The Wemmicks were small wooden people, carved by a wood-worker named Eli....Each Wemmick was different. Some had big noses, others had large eyes. Some were tall and others were short, some skinny, some fat, some handsome or pretty, some not....But all were made by the same carver and all lived in the village. And all day, every day the Wemmicks did the same thing. They gave each other stickers. Each Wemmick had a box of golden star stickers and a box of grey dot stickers. Up and down the streets people spent their days sticking stars or dots on one another. The pretty ones, those with smooth woods and fine paint always got stars. But if the wood was rough or the paint chipped, the Wemmicks gave dots. The talented ones got stars, too. Some could lift big sticks far above their head or jump over tall boxes. Still others knew big words or could sing pretty songs. Everyone gave them stars.

Some Wemmicks had stars all over them. Every time they got a star it made them feel so good. It made them want to do something else, to get another star. Others, though, could do little and they got dots. Punchinello was one of these. He tried to jump high, like the others but he always fell. And when he fell, the others would gather around him and give him dots. Sometimes when he fell his wood got scratched so that the people would give him more dots....

"He deserves a lot of dots," the wooden people would agree with one another. "He is not a good wooden person." After hearing this so many times, Punchinello believed them. "I'm not a good Wemmick," he would say.[5]

As the story goes, Punchinello eventually met his maker, Eli, who told him to stop worrying about the dots that everyone else had put on him. All that mattered, Eli said, was what he thought about him; and he thought that Punchinello was very special.

Punchinello laughed. "Me—special? Why, I can't walk fast; I can't jump; my paint is peeling. Why do I matter to you?" Eli looked at Punchinello, put his hands on those small wooden shoulders and said "Because you are mine. That is why you matter to me."[6]

I am a "Punchinello." I have lived most of my life feeling as though I have dots all over me because of my same-sex attractions. Sometimes I try to jump high, but every day, one way or another, I fall. And when I fall, I get scratched, I get hurt, I get disappointed, and I feel like I've let God down. It's easy for me to think I am a failure and that I will never get it right. There is nothing, and I mean nothing, that has caused me to have more dots than my same-gender attractions. And sadly, I confess that I've put most of them on myself.

I'm guilty of having listened to the lies of Satan far too often and allowing the devil to put dots all over me. The Bible does say that Satan's native tongue is lying. He is called the "accuser," and in my life he has done his job well. I hear Satan whispering in my ear:

- "I'll never change."

- "I can't be loved by God or others being attracted to the same sex."

- "I am evil."

- "There is something wrong with me that I can't change this."

- "God has made a mistake."

- "I'm failing as a disciple having thoughts like that."

- "Is there really any hope? Why kid myself? Why not just go and live the way I want to: Be "gay," accept it; it's the only way I'll truly be happy."

- "I've been through this too many times already. I might as well give up. It is only a matter of time before I'm back to my old ways of life anyway."

- "I'm missing out; if I could go and do the things I really want, I would be fulfilled."

- "I'm not really a Christian; I'm not really saved."

As a Christian who lives with unwanted same-gender attractions, I've had every one of those thoughts and more many times over the years; and yes, for those wondering, I've been to therapy.

This whispering technique of Satan's (to mask his thoughts as our own) is a trick that goes back a long way. In Genesis the Hebrew word translated as "serpent" in the Garden of Eden account is interpreted as "hisser" or "whisperer." He whispers lies into our ears like he did with Eve. I know he does to everyone, but for those who suffer homoerotic attractions, the devil deserves overtime pay.

Because of our human weaknesses in this broken and fallen world, Satan loves to try to convince us that we are all losers, that all of us are "Wemmicks" worthy of only dots. But it's not true. As with Eli, the woodworker in Max Lucado's children's book, all that matters is what our Maker thinks about us, and it just so happens he thinks that each one of us is very special. We may wonder occasionally why, because there are times when, like Punchinello, we can't walk fast, our paint peels and we keep tripping and falling. But when that occurs, our Maker always reassures us by lovingly putting his hands on our shoulders and saying, "I love you because you are mine, and that is why you matter to me."

Resources

1. Joe Dallas, *Desires in Conflict: Hope for Men Who Struggle with Sexual Identity* (Eugene, OR: Harvest House, 2003).
2. Alan Chambers, *Leaving Homosexuality* (Eugene, OR: Harvest House, 2011).

Chapter Two Endnotes

1. Joe Dallas, *Desires in Conflict: Hope for Men Who Struggle with Sexual Identity*. (Eugene, OR: Harvest House, 2003), 23.

2. Wade Meredith, "What Happens to Your Body When You Drink a Coke Right Now?" http://www.healthbolt.net/2006/12/08/what-happens-to -your-body-if-you-drink-a-coke-right-now/.

3. George Strait, "Poison" (MCA Records, 2011).

4. "Living Water Part 1," http://www.settingcaptivesfree.com.

5. Max Lucado, *You Are Special* (New York, NY: Scholastic Inc, 1997) 7–15.

6. Ibid., 27.

Chapter Three

Practicals for Helping
Same-Sex Attracted Christians

It's not who you are; it's how you are.
                    —14-year-old boy from my son's hockey team

Satan is not the brightest light in the harbor; for you inland dwellers out there, I apologize for the lighthouse analogy. The Atlantic Ocean is literally a five-minute drive from my house, therefore I'm surrounded by them—but you get my point, right? Shall I go on so that everyone feels included? What I am getting at is—when it comes to the devil—he's a few screws short of a hardware store. He's got 4-wheel drive but only three of them are spinning, is a few yards short of a touchdown, has only one oar in the water, is a few Bradys short of a bunch and has lost contact with the mother ship; his antenna doesn't pick up all the channels and he's one board member short of a quorum. If you gave him a penny for his thoughts, you'd get change. He'd lose a debate with a doorknob; he's not the sharpest knife in the drawer; the elevator doesn't go all the way to the top; the cheese has slipped off the cracker—and I really could go on.

So now that I've pulled in all you carpenters who drive 4-wheel-drive trucks, love throwing a football and who, in the evenings, secretly watch reruns of the Brady Bunch and Star Trek on your old black-and-white antenna television sets before heading out to a board meeting, I'll continue. Why am I being so hard on old Beelzebub? Because, when it comes to trying to trick us, lie to us and cause us to sin, he really doesn't have all that much of an imagination. Of course, I am not unaware of Jude 1:9, where we are told that even the archangel Michael, when arguing with the devil, "did not dare to bring a slanderous accusation against him." I am cognizant of that danger and certainly would not want to tread where even angels refuse to go—but I also don't believe that I've even come close to making blasphemous accusations against the Prince of Demons. Rather, I am just speaking to his lack of ingenuity when it comes to temptation. I mean, we all struggle with the same "stuff," don't we? He's been throwing the same kind of enticements and temptations at humankind since the days that Adam and Even strolled nude through the garden.

It's not like the devil keeps coming up with new temptations with which to lure us. Sure, due to technological advances—as if we seem intent on proving Romans 1:30 true—humans have become good at inventing new ways of sinning. But at the core of it all, Satan comes at us with the same old junk: lust, greed, deceit, slander, gossip, anger, fits of rage, hatred, overindulgence, idolatry, jealousy, pride, et cetera, et cetera—am I right? It does not matter how long you've been a disciple—five minutes or fifty years—every single one of us is susceptible to Satan's old bag of tricks. If he were to catch any of us at exactly the right moment—when our guard is down—there is not one of us who could truthfully claim that we've not sinned in any of these areas to one degree or another.

They're Everywhere

I suppose that's why I'm always amused to hear Christians speak with such astonishment when they come to the realization that there are disciples who are tempted with homosexuality. At times they even sin in their astonishment, and by that I'm not amused. It creates an environment that is unfortunate for those who are same-sex attracted; they often feel unable to be transparent about any struggle in the one place they should feel the safest to share such information—the church. Isn't it a place full of sinners, all equally in need of the blood of Jesus to keep us clean? No Christian should think for a minute that this issue does not affect their local congregation, for I have counseled, talked to and cried with disciples from literally all over the world who come from a homosexual past and who still live with unwanted homoerotic attractions.

Some of these people are your evangelists, church leaders, elders and small-group leaders. They serve in your Sunday children's programs, lead songs, play in your band and teach lessons in your services. They are in your singles, married, campus and teen ministries.

At every service you sit beside them in church and hug them in fellowship; you eat with them in your homes. They are your friends and people whom you love and respect dearly. I know this to be true, for I've talked to them. They are male and female and come from North, Central and South America; Europe; Asia; the Middle East and Africa. Other than the Arctic and Antarctica, I've personally counseled Christians who live with same-sex attractions from every continent on the globe, and no doubt I will hear from the North and South Poles some day in the future. Yet most in our pews don't know that the person with whom they are worshipping and whom they call "brother" or "sister" bears a story of fear, hurt, isolation and confusion that most might never appreciate.

How Many Christians Are Same-Sex Attracted?

To answer the question of how many people in the church are same-gender attracted, we must first take a brief look at what the latest studies tell us about how many people identify themselves as "homosexual" or "bisexual" in the overall population. You may have read or heard the common misconception first reported by Alfred Kinsey, one of the very first scientists to conduct large-scale scientific surveys into human sexuality and who authored *Sexual Behavior in the Human Male* in 1948 and *Sexual Behavior in the Human Female* in 1953. According to him, ten percent of the population is homosexual or gay.[1]

This number is still widely held to be true although the majority of researchers in this field dispute those findings:

> Researchers rarely discuss just how deeply flawed Kinsey's data appeared to be. For a study such as Kinsey's to produce data from which we could generalize to the whole population, the sample under study would have to be roughly representative of that general population....But Kinsey seems to have ignored the need to keep his sample reflective of the American population. It appears as though Kinsey's sample of males was skewed

because he oversampled a variety of groups....And curiously, every example of oversampling appears to have increased the likelihood of finding a higher incidence of nontraditional sexual practices.[2] ...Two sample distortions are the most shocking: First, Kinsey drastically oversampled prison inmates....Second, Kinsey drastically oversampled members of gay-affirming organizations.[3]

So let's forget Kinsey and this 10% figure altogether, as that number is clearly not accurate. What percentage is most correct?

While almost impossible to truly pinpoint accurately, based on the most recent studies provided, it is generally agreed that the figure stands between three and four percent of the population. A study provided by a U.S. government survey reports that the number of adults between the ages of eighteen to forty-five who identify themselves as either "homosexual" or "bisexual" stands at 4%,[4] and a 2011 study published by UCLA School of Law puts the figure at 3.8%.[5] It would be a mistake to assume that our congregations do not reflect the diversity of our cultures, considering that our memberships are made up of individuals who have been plucked from the very world from which this data is derived.

It would also be incorrect to deduce (and I have heard the argument) that because so many in the church are second- and third-generation children of church members (in other words, they "grew up" in the church) that this percentage would be lower because these children would have been raised in a Christian home—an environment that teaches the biblical sexual ethic—thereby decreasing the possibility that children from Christian homes would be same-sex attracted. To accept that argument would mean ignoring the following two realities: First, at its core, same-sex attraction is not more of a moral dilemma than it is a by-product of an individual suffering emotional deficiencies left unmet in childhood; this can occur in a Christian home just as it can in a non-Christian home. Second, there is not always rhyme or reason as to why someone is homosexually attracted.

While it is true that over a hundred years of research has shown that the common denominator for both male and female same-sex attraction is driven by sexual trauma and/or emotional and relational deficits experienced during adolescence, there are same-sex-attracted kids who grew up in safe, loving, well-adjusted Christian homes who simply did not experience the pattern normally attributed to this trait. Therefore, it is safe to say that on average, three to four percent of the men and women in your home congregation are most likely same-sex attracted. Do the math for your own home congregation.

I Know It's Intimidating

Humbly understanding that all of us are a mixture of glory and tragedy mingled together, how can Christians practically help this small but very important and needed demographic in our churches? It is true that our brothers and sisters need the benefit of focused attention, encouragement and support. Many have left the church because they didn't feel like they could be truly authentic, open and transparent with their lives for fear of being rebuffed. Those who stay faithful often do so silently for the same fear of rejection. Whether those fears have been genuine or more perceived—as was in my case—is not the point. The point is that the stakes are high and understanding what works and what doesn't when offering support is critical to the success of helping these men and women navigate their Christian lives. Hence, I applaud you for reading this book and I congratulate the leadership teams of local congregations who have been eager to educate themselves on this confusing issue.

I fully recognize and appreciate the years of pastoral care that our church leaders and elders have faithfully provided to their congregants. As an evangelist, I know what it's like to have to be the jack-of-all-trades in a church—somehow being expected to know all the answers to all the problems that come your way. It seems that because one is in the full-time ministry, they are supposed to be an expert on every conceivable topic, which of course is just not possible. I know also that many feel a sense of intimidation when it comes to helping someone who comes from a homosexual past. I know that the topic is messy and awkward to discuss, and complex. Therefore, I offer this chapter on what every Christian can do and what kind of attitude they should employ when attempting to assist disciples who live with unwanted same-gender attractions.

Genuine Affection Moves the Heart

It is incredible how genuine affection will move the heart. To get there, though, I've got to tell you this true story because it so well illustrates the first and foremost essential entity that must be owned by every Christian who longs to help others. For those of you who do not come from Canada, I need to explain a little bit about our culture to you. Because this country spends the majority of the year under a blanket of ice and snow, it only stands to reason that ice hockey is the most popular sport here. The sport's most renowned professional athlete is a Canadian by the name of Wayne Gretzky. He was, without a doubt, the greatest player to ever lace up a pair of skates. During his nineteen-year professional career he broke sixty-one records, was named the National Hockey League's most valuable player ten times, and led his team to winning the Stanley Cup (hockey's most cherished prize) four times. He was also recently voted one of the "Top Ten Greatest Canadians of All Time."[6] As great as Wayne Gretzky was (his nickname actually is "The Great One"), my story is not about him, but rather about his father, Walter.

Walter became a household name across Canada as the story became known of how he passed on his passion for hockey to his son, Wayne. He taught the boy how to strategically think several steps ahead of everyone else on the ice, giving his son the tools he used to become the greatest player of all time. He is known as "Canada's Hockey Dad." In 1991, Walter suffered a brain aneurysm from which he nearly died. Although he survived, the aneurysm resulted in a permanent twenty-year year lapse in memory of the early 1970s to the early 1990s—the period of time when he would have witnessed his son win all of those championships and break those sixty-one records. However, after years of intense physiotherapy, hockey's most famous father not only recovered, he has since risen to become one of the greatest ambassadors for numerous charities across North America. Walter Gretzky first became known because he is Wayne's father, but it is his caring heart and zeal for those less privileged and the down and out that have made him such a popular speaker.

Walter Gretzky was recently in my hometown of Halifax, Nova Scotia to help raise money for the Salvation Army. A good friend of mine, Ron, whose son played on my son's hockey team, worked in public relations for the Salvation Army and organized the fundraiser. Hundreds stood in line to get their opportunity to meet Walter. It became obvious that much more time would have to be scheduled for the event because he was so intent on signing an autograph for every single person and holding a conversation with each as well. His gentle and caring nature was obvious—especially for the residents who were living at the Salvation Army.

> Perhaps Walter's greatest enthusiasm came when he had his picture taken with one of the new graduates of the 12-step addictions program. "Wow! This is fantastic! Way to go!" he exclaimed in typical exuberance, leaving all to think the achievement was akin to a game-seven winning goal in the Stanley Cup finals.[7]

While in Halifax, Mr. Gretzky refused to stay in a hotel, preferring instead to stay with Ron, his wife and his kids. He had such an incredible impact on this family that when it came time to take Walter to the airport, their son got choked up and didn't want to see him go. As he later explained to his father, "Dad, it's not who he is, it's how he is."[8] It is incredible how genuine affection, warmth and kindness will move and touch so many, isn't it?

Who We Are Drawn To

I think this is how Jesus was. To the leper whom Jesus reached out and touched when he most likely had not felt the stroke of another person's hand in years, I'm confident it was not *who* Jesus was, but *how* Jesus was. To the woman caught in the act of adultery and who desperately needed someone with compassion to step in and save her from a group of self-righteous hypocrites who were eager to kill someone that day—it was not only *who* Jesus was, but *how* Jesus was. And what of the woman who braved the contemptuous, scornful looks of the "respectable" people who gathered in the courtyard of Simon, the Pharisee, to hear Jesus teach, just so that she could pour perfume on his feet?

Before she could get the jar open, tears of gratitude poured down her cheeks and onto Jesus' feet. Simon wondered how Jesus could let this sinful woman touch him and do these things. He saw her as an "object" that was disgusting and detestable because of her gross misdeeds. Jesus, however, saw a woman who was yearning to be freed from her past: who longed to be forgiven, who had been abused by a cruel and heartless world, and who was treated with equal cruelty by the religious establishment. And while this woman remains unnamed and we know nothing else of her life, she stands as a testament of what it means to be drawn to Jesus—not just because of who Jesus is, but because of *how* he is.

From my early teens to the present time, I have been under the influence of numerous ministers, evangelists, elders, deacons, and many other leaders all with varying titles and levels of responsibility. They all worked hard, and I am grateful for the impact they have had on my life. But there are very few to whom I was willing to give my heart, with whom I was willing to be open and transparent with regard to my homosexual past and same-gender attractions, whom I allowed to know the real me. These few did not impress me with their stunning oratory skills or reputation or level of education or any other ministerial credentials. Rather, I was drawn to these men because they were kind, compassionate and sensitive and did not think too highly of themselves. They were eager to love and accept me even in my very broken state. I was drawn to them not because of who they were, but because of *how* they were.

One of the priorities of Strength in Weakness Ministries is to encourage same-gender-attracted brothers and sisters to be open and transparent with one or two spiritually mature and trusted individuals in their home congregation. I cannot overstate how transformational having these kinds of relationships has been for me. To be loved, to be believed in and to be supported by brothers who are my friends (even though they know who I was and who I am) is nothing but a gift from God!

When Isolation Is Considered the Better Option

But I dare say that I am in the minority of same-gender-attracted Christians around the world who develop and utilize these kinds of accountability relationships. For many in our congregations around the world there are possible serious consequences when it comes to transparency due to the way different cultures and local laws deal with homosexuality. For Christians who come from the continent of Africa and from within the Middle East and other predominantly Muslim cultures, one can be incarcerated or even executed for being involved in homosexuality; isolation often seems by far the better option compared to transparency and confession.

In 2011 the International Lesbian, Gay, Bisexual, Trans and Intersex Association completed a comprehensive study of global laws on homosexuality, and the research showed that seventy-six countries still persecute and prosecute people on the grounds of their sexual orientation and seven still punish same-sex acts with death. Church leaders, elders and those responsible for supplying pastoral care in these countries especially need to be able to separate what the world calls illegal and treats with cruelty but is simply a part of the broken human condition (same-sex attraction) from what the Bible calls sin (homosexuality). They then need to proceed with extreme caution and confidentiality, recognizing the possible dangers ahead should anyone else discover that there are homosexually attracted Christians in their fellowship.

For the disciple who resides within Western-civilized countries where homosexuality is not illegal (Western Europe, the Americas and Australasia), being transparent about their homosexual struggles can also be a distressing event—many have already spent the majority of their adult lives bearing the brunt of cruel jokes, being subjected to offensive language and being called derogatory names. Some have been completely disowned by their parents, friends and other loved ones. Still others have faced physical persecution and been wrongly stereotyped, often considered as less-than-second-rate people.

I remember so clearly the inner turmoil I suffered while trying to build the courage to tell my minister that I was "gay." It was absolutely terrifying. It was one thing to be rejected and made fun of by a judgmental world, but to fear that I might be unwanted by my brothers and sisters was too much to endure. I was sure that some in the church would pull away from me, rebuff my friendship and make unfair assumptions about my life and character, and that I might even be asked to leave for good because of it. This was a fear that was not restricted to the beginning of my Christian journey, but unfortunately one that I held onto for the first nineteen years of my Christian experience. In fact even today, after speaking so publicly and broadly about my homosexual attractions, I still suffer tremendous amounts of anxiety and insecurity before stepping up to the pulpit of churches where I've been invited to speak, knowing that I'm about to confess to hundreds or thousands of people that I'm a same-sex-attracted disciple.

To the church's credit, I have seen that my fears have been largely unfounded and based much more on my doubts and insecurities than reality; and truthfully, I have felt the love, acceptance and compassion I so long for in the church. There have been a few exceptions of course, but overall in the life of Guy Hammond, the bride of Christ has proven to be what Jesus intended it to be after all. With that being said, building trust is crucial in helping same-sex-attracted Christians.

It's Not Unlike a Doctor-Patient Relationship

My father spent most of his life a very ill man. While so many difficult memories flood my mind with all he suffered, one evening in particular stands out to me. On this night, the throbbing between his temples was so severe and with his bedroom being up a flight of stairs, he simply did not own the strength necessary to scale the steps to his bed. Instead, he was forced to get out of his La-Z-Boy recliner and crawl slowly to the middle of the living room floor, where he collapsed. I had already turned off most of the lights in the house as my dad had instructed me to, as even the slightest beam of illumination was like a bullet through his eyes. He suffered from migraines—not the kind that could be taken away by over-the-counter drugs. Even more potent prescriptions like Percodan, 222, injections of morphine and including different combinations of narcotics and barbiturates all had little effect.

Constant visits to hospital emergency wards (literally almost weekly as I grew up), acupuncture, massage therapy and whatever else was prescribed and tried all proved ineffective through the years. In fact, I literally do not recollect a day from as far back as my mind will allow me to travel, when he did not have to undergo the agonizing pounding that started just above the left eye, spread to his temples, across the top of his head and then down to the base of his skull. While the pain was almost continuous, during the majority of days he carried the vigor necessary to get through his day-to-day responsibilities. But that was not the case on this night. Possible relief seemed nonexistent and hopeless. There was no use in calling an ambulance as I had on other evenings when I was alone with him and completely powerless as a child to help him. There was simply nothing that the medical profession had to offer that would give him relief.

As the tears streamed down his face, he asked me to get his Bible.

I was twelve at the time, maybe thirteen. When I returned, my dad had me sit beside him on the floor and read over and over again the only soothing words that would provide comfort for him—the twenty-third Psalm: "Yeah, though I walk through the valley of the shadow of death, I will fear no evil, for thou art with me" (KJV). I'll never forget that night. That evening and so many others are burned into my memory, like when he would be preaching and in the middle of his sermon would, on occasion, have to interrupt it and apologetically excuse himself from the pulpit, and then ask the song leader to lead the congregation in a few hymns while he lay on the front pew trying to regain the strength to carry on. Or all the hours—hundreds of them I'm sure—sitting in emergency waiting rooms until the wee hours of the morning when he was given yet another needle for the pain.

When a Good Bedside Manner Is Necessary

It's funny how certain things stand out to me all these years later, such as those doctors and nurses who were thoughtful, empathetic and considerate—those who had an amazing "bedside manner." But then, there were the few who would have put Dr. House to shame (you know who I'm referring to if you've ever watched the U.S. television series called *House*, where the irritable physician goes out of his way to prove that "compassionate medical care" can be an oxymoron). I'll never forget these individuals because of how cold, indifferent and insensitive they were as they administered their "help." I've never personally been ill enough to need assistance like that and prayerfully never will be, but I could see how the completely unsympathetic attitudes that some displayed hurt my dad, making him regret that he had come for the help to begin with. Somehow, it was worth putting up with even the severe pain he suffered, if only to not have to be put through the indignity at the hands of these "caregivers" who did not care about him and many of whom even questioned the severity of his suffering.

Not being a doctor, nurse or any part of the health care profession myself, I can't imagine how difficult these jobs must be. I'm sure that all day long having to assist people who are suffering can make one weary. The times must come, especially after a long shift, when it becomes difficult to keep feeling the pain of others in such a way that you could continue to be empathetic in every interaction. But to the person who is ill and feeling alone, afraid, vulnerable and unsure of what's going to happen next, the bedside manner of the attending health care professional is necessary because it comforts and encourages the patient. When you're sensitive to how the person is feeling, your vocal tones, body language and calming presence can put them at ease and let them know that you are there to help. Someone with poor bedside manner ends up leaving the patient worried, concerned and anxious.

Jesus, who was of course the ultimate physician, had a tremendous bedside manner. He was always sensitive, concerned and aware of the disease with which the person suffered. He was also aware of how vulnerable, afraid and insecure that person would be feeling. One of the most moving and touching stories in all of Scripture provides us with an example of Jesus' incredible bedside manner. In Mark 7:31–35, as Jesus was making his way through town, he was presented with a man who was both deaf and mute. Read this short story, and look at Jesus' wonderful example of how to treat people when they are in despair:

> Then Jesus left the vicinity of Tyre and went through Sidon, down to the Sea of Galilee and into the region of the Decapolis. There some people brought to him a man who was deaf and could hardly talk, and they begged him to place his hand on the man.
>
> *After he took him aside, away from the crowd, Jesus put his fingers into the man's ears. Then he spit and touched the man's tongue. He looked up to heaven and with a deep sigh said to him, "Ephphatha!" (which means, "Be opened!").* At this, the man's ears were opened, his tongue was loosened and he began to speak plainly. (emphasis added)

Not being one who has suffered such physical infirmity, I did some minor research on what it is like to be deaf. I found a letter written by Ludwig van Beethoven in October of 1808 to his brother Carl where he pours out his heart on the different levels of emotional pain that he suffered from being unable to hear. He used words like "solitude," "misunderstood," "no relaxation in society," "entirely alone," "an outcast," "fear," "awkward," "suspicious," "embarrassed" and "confused."[9] These are just some of the feelings a deaf person lives with. So what of Jesus' bedside manner with this man?

The Lord did something quite beautiful. He took the man by the hand, led him off to the side where he was alone with him and *healed him in private*. No crowds, no chaos, no show. Here was a man who had lived a life of being misunderstood, who could not relax in society, who felt entirely alone, an outcast, awkward, suspicious, embarrassed and confused. Jesus in his caring way knew this, and so as to not turn this healing into some kind of grandiose show where the feelings of insecurity would only be amplified, Jesus took him aside to be alone with him and treated him in private. To Jesus, this poor man was not a show, but a man who had feelings and emotions and who needed to be treated with both respect and sensitivity.[10] Jesus wanted to calm his fears and let him know that he was there to help and not to hurt.

Then, in a continuing fashion of heightened concern for this gentleman, Jesus put his fingers in the man's ears, spit and touched the man's tongue. The ancient world had a curious belief in the healing power of saliva.[11] Jesus of course knew that spit had no healing properties, but because the deaf man believed that it did, the Lord, in his gentle and thoughtful way, administered an ancient form of healing so that the man knew that Jesus was there to heal him and would not harm him. Time and time again throughout Scripture Jesus displayed the ability to be thoughtful and understanding of the frailties and vulnerabilities of the human psyche and soul.

When Jesus met a leper who begged for healing he not only healed him, but first, in a tender display of human affection, reached out and touched the man. The leper most likely had not felt the stroke of another person's hand in years, but Jesus had a tremendous bedside manner. What does this have to do with helping homosexuals or Christians who are same-gender attracted? Everything.

The Lepers Among Us

A nonprofit, faith-based organization in England dedicated to speaking out against pro-gay activism throughout Great Britain and Ireland holds an annual conference called "Lepers Among Us." Putting all possible good intent aside, I wonder: Is it conceivable to be any more insensitive? I doubt it, as in my humble estimation, it is hardly the kind of bridge-building language needed in order to engage with the Gay,

Lesbian, Bisexual, Transgendered (GLBT) community in a manner that would encourage helpful dialogue.

The title of this group's conference has garnered widespread condemnation by the media throughout Europe. Aside from its tactlessness, the conference name has touched an open nerve in the gay community, mostly because many homosexual men and women have often felt like they are indeed the lepers of our generation. Just as lepers of centuries ago were to be avoided, considered unclean and forced to live in segregated communities, homosexuals also have suffered the wounds of often being avoided, considered unclean and forced into segregated social communities. Just as Jesus was willing to reach out and touch the leper and in so doing went against all cultural norms of the time so as to convey mercy, love and compassion, disciples of Jesus must be willing to do the same with homosexuals today. In other words, Christians cannot allow a sinful world to dictate to Jesus' church how we will treat others.

It is important to take into account how same-sex-attracted individuals coming into the church often feel as we consider who we will be to these people and the kind of bedside manner we will exhibit when trying to help. I can tell you that in my personal journey as a homosexually attracted man in the church, regardless of the tremendous victories that I have experienced in overcoming my sinful past and in learning to live successfully as a Christian who still suffers homoerotic attractions, I have lived most days feeling different from everyone else and like an outsider. For sure, many of the insecurities that I have experienced have been self-inflicted and based unfairly on what I feared would happen if Christians were to learn of my same-sex attractions, different from what actually did occur when I became transparent with my sinful nature. But in truth, I have heard some pretty ridiculous and insensitive comments emanate from the mouths of well-meaning Christians over the years.

The lessons I have taken from this and freely pass on to other same-sex-attracted disciples is that these situations are opportunities to provide compassion and forgiveness to those who would say such hurtful things, appreciating that they simply did not know what they were doing. As I mentioned earlier, when my dad sought help from the medical profession and came into contact with someone with a terrible bedside manner, somehow even the severe pain was worth putting up with if only to be spared the indignity of his caregivers seemingly not caring.

Sometimes I've felt the same. If you can keep that in mind when jumping in to offer spiritual counsel and friendship, it will go a long way in determining your bedside manner. Go in knowing that same-gender-attracted Christians, just as Beethoven who was deaf, have spent much of their time living in solitude, feeling misunderstood, alone, awkward, ashamed and embarrassed.

Here then are six practical things you can do to help same-sex-attracted disciples:

1. Create an environment where it is *easy* to be open and transparent.

When mentoring a same-gender-attracted friend, remember that sins and temptations will be confessed to you that you have never personally experienced or even considered, things that you may personally deem repugnant. Jesus was no doubt repulsed by the sins of others as well, but he never allowed that to transfer over to how he treated the person. The individual you are helping needs to know that they can freely confess and discuss *anything* with you, without you pulling away or rejecting them. In fact, there will never be a time when they need to feel your love and acceptance more than when they have laid their heart out on the table like this. They will only feel free to return to you again if they truly believe that you love them unconditionally and that you provide a safe place for them to talk freely and openly.

The unconditional love of Jesus drew people to push through crowds to get to him because they knew that with him, they would not be judged or condemned (John 8:10). In Jesus we find safety and security, not judgment and condemnation. Jesus himself did not come to judge the world but to save it. All that Jesus expected was repentance. Let this be our attitude as well.

2. Be confidential.

If I had any inkling that the people I was being transparent with were either gossiping or passing along private information that I was confessing—that would have ended the relationship immediately. You simply must be a *safe and secure* confidante. If you feel like you need assistance and would like to pull someone else in, you must ask or tell the person you are helping *first*. If, in your opinion, your friend is doing something that is hurting him- or herself or someone else (or after a period of time just not repenting), then go to a spiritually mature individual to get help. But even then, do not do so without informing your friend first that you are doing this. In my opinion, it should be done as an *absolute last resort*.

3. Have a conviction that homosexuality is *not* the worst of all sins.

Although it has often been treated as such by many Christians, the Bible does not single out homosexuality as a "unique sin" that God hates more than any other. While actively being involved in homosexuality is clearly a sin, to God it is just as evil to be involved in stealing, being greedy, lying, or any kind of sexual sin by heterosexuals (1 Corinthians 6: 9–11). We all need to have an appreciation for the fact that all Christians have their own unique issues, sinful natures and temptations to work through. Many disciples (regardless of sexual orientation) show their different areas of brokenness through sexual dysfunction. Sexual brokenness is hardly exclusive to the homosexual or same-gender attracted (see 1 Corinthians 5:9–13, 6:9–20; Matthew 5:27–28).

4. Understand that being attracted to the same sex is not a choice.

It is not my desire to delve into causation right now, as we will address whether or not there is a genetic cause for homosexuality in the upcoming chapter "Answering the Most Often Asked Questions About Homosexuality." I touch on it as well in the chapter "Practical Help for Parents," so I'll just now ask you to take it from me, a Christian man of twenty-five years who has been same-gender attracted almost as far back as I can recall, that I never consciously chose this, nor have I ever met anyone who did. With the shame, embarrassment, isolation and rejection often involved for those who live with this daily, who on earth would actually *choose* this, given the choice? I became aware of my homosexual feelings when I hit puberty, just like others became aware of their heterosexual feelings when they reached puberty. It was not a conscious choice; it just was. So do not assume that homosexuality is a consciously chosen sexual preference; it isn't.

That being the case, let me suggest that when communicating with a same-sex-attracted disciple or even with parents of same-gender-attracted children, words of correction and assistance be given with humility, gentleness and hesitancy. Please do not think that this is something that someone can change by trying harder. Homosexuality is the result of a combination of multiple factors and contributing influences. It would be wrong for anyone to suggest that it is something that can be turned on or off at will. Please also do not promise healing is possible provided that someone just has more faith, prays more or simply repents. Although I do believe that God is capable of intervening in a person's life and changing unwanted same-gender attractions, he also often chooses not to, which is fine, for having a heterosexual orientation is hardly a prerequisite to salvation.

I realize these are confusing issues, but take heart; whenever anyone has tried to help me, I never expected them to have all the answers. I just needed to trust them and know they cared. Help others to rejoice in the freedom that they have every day; no longer do they have to be slaves to their emotions and temptations; they have the freedom to choose another path for their lives by following Jesus. Help them in their daily walk to be self-controlled, prayerful and obedient to the Lord—regardless of what their emotions, hormones and feelings are telling them. Help them to know that their value and worth to God and the church and to you as a friend is not based on their sexual attractions. Help them to live holy lives.

5. Have realistic expectations.

The same-sex-attracted Christian you are trying to help will be just like you. They will have their good days and their bad days. There will be times when they will be strong in their faith and other times when they are weak. There will be times when they sin in their hearts and minds by giving in to homosexual fantasies and old thought patterns, and some will even act out homosexually in a physical way, after which they will need spiritual counsel and guidance as they repent. Remember that while Jesus may have taken away their sins, their attractions to the same gender and the struggle to live righteously in this broken and fallen world will have remained. That is all right, because the goal that Jesus has for them is not that they live a problem-free, temptation-free existence, but rather that they have a relationship with him.

6. Teach them what a healthy same-gender friendship is supposed to be like.

Men and women who come from a homosexual past and who live with unwanted same-sex attractions, when they first join the church, most often do not know how to build and sustain a healthy, nonsexual friendship with another member of the same gender. Speaking as a man who has struggled with this himself, I can tell you that I found it difficult to find acceptance or know how to relate with my own gender. In the first several years that I was in the church especially, I would often feel isolated and insecure around other men, feeling like I didn't measure up among my peers. When I first became a disciple, I really didn't know how to build a strong, healthy, pure and godly friendship with another guy.

The world of men: how they talked and related to each other and how they communicated both verbally and physically with one another, was so foreign to me. Over the years, I have tried to fit in and relate, but even after all this time I confess that I still often find it awkward. What has helped the most, however, has been having spiritual men welcoming and including me in their activities and treating me as they would any other guy, allowing me to learn from them as I watch them interact with their friends and peers. This has helped me tremendously in learning how to fit in and build godly male relationships.

If you can capture the heart of what I've discussed in this chapter by being one who has a sensitive and caring bedside manner as Christ did, you will be incredibly successful in helping these wonderful men and women in your life. The goal is to provide a safe, loving and protective environment for these children of God, not a place of condemnation. I pray you will be like our Savior—who was able to look below the surface and see people who were yearning to be freed from the past—as you grow in your relationships with one another. Only then will they be more impressed with *how* you are than with *who* you are.

Resources

1. Sy Rogers, *Lessons Learned: Insights for Redeeming the Sexual Generation*, two CDs (Fort Lauderdale, FL: Worthy Creations, 2003).

2. Joe Dallas, *The Game Plan: The Men's 30-Day Strategy for Attaining Sexual Integrity* (Nashville, TN: Thomas Nelson Inc, 2005).

Chapter Three Endnotes

1. Alfred C. Kinsey and Wardel B. Pomeroy, *Sexual Behavior in the Human Male* (Philadelphia, PA: Saunders, 1948).

2. Further study on this is discussed in Judith A. Reisman and Edward W. Eichel, *Kinsey, Sex and Fraud: The Indoctrination of a People* (Lafayette, LA: Huntington House, 1990).

3. Stanton L. Jones and Mark A. Yarhouse, *Homosexuality: The Use of Scientific Research in the Church's Moral Debate* (Downers Grove, IL: InterVarsity Press, 2000), 36–37.

4. Gary Gates of the Williams Institute on Sexual Orientation Law and Public Policy at the UCLA School of Law, interview by Ramone Johnson, 2008, http://www.gaylife.about.com.

5. Gary J. Gates, "How Many People Are Lesbian, Gay, Bisexual and Transgender?" April, 2011, http://williamsinstitute.law.ucla.edu/research /census-lgbt-demographics-studies/how-many-people-are-lesbian-gay -bisexual-and-transgender/.

6. "The Greatest Canadian," 2004, http://www.cbc.ca/greatest/top_ten/.

7. Ron Zima, "Salvation Army Stories and Pictures from the Maritimes" May 21, 2008, maritimesonline.blogspot.com/.

8. Ibid.

9. Ludvig van Beethoven, "Immortal Glory," in *A Beethoven Reader*, ed. F. V. Grunfeld (New York, NY: Columbia Masterworks, 1972), 13.

10. William Barclay, *The Gospel of Mark*, 3rd ed. (Edinburgh, Scotland: St. Andrew Press, 1953), 182–83.

11. Ibid.

Chapter Four

Practical Help
for Husbands and Wives

"A successful marriage requires falling in love many times,
always with the same person."
—Mignon McLaughlin, American journalist

I experienced a miracle. It was February 23, 1991, just an average and nondescript day in Toronto, Canada. It was cold, although surprisingly warmer than usual for an afternoon in mid-February. Beyond that small fact, however, if you were able to ask the approximately three million inhabitants who lived in that city at the time if anything stood out to them that day, the majority would most likely say "No." Most in that city were not cognizant of it, but at two o'clock that afternoon, a miracle occurred. The extraordinary event was observed by about one hundred folks I'd say, and to most gathered, I suppose even they did not fully appreciate the significance of the moment—often what occurs when a miracle is performed. But I knew.

It was very clear to me that in our presence, God was performing a miracle, something completely out of the ordinary, something so unique that only his blessing would make it work. The miracle was the marriage of Guy Hammond, a man who had lived an active gay life for years and who was still attracted to the same gender, to Cathy Hamilton, a beautiful, wonderful, spiritual and amazing heterosexually attracted woman. There had been a time in my life when never, never, never did I think it possible that I could be married to a woman—much less successfully and happily—not ever. Yet, as of the writing of this chapter, I have been married to Cathy for almost twenty-two years, and I have done pretty well in this area, considering the circumstances, if I don't mind saying so myself!

Not that Cathy and I haven't had our challenges, and I have certainly been far from the perfect husband. We love each other beyond words, have a frequent and healthy physical relationship and we enjoy spending time together. Sharing our lives with one another has made us so incredibly happy that it's easy to see God's love and wisdom in uniting us in this way. If you were to ask my wife if in this marriage she feels loved, special and taken care of, she would give an enthusiastic "Yes!" If you were to ask her if she had any regrets about marrying a man who is same-sex attracted, I'm confident she would give a fervent, "No!" (I know this because I asked her just before writing this chapter).

Welcome to the Club!

If you are the spouse of a same-sex-attracted husband or wife, let me welcome you to God's school of learning! This is an amazing chance you have been blessed with to grow in your faith. What an incredible opportunity you have been given to imitate his heart of compassion, sensitivity and unconditional love. I have been the recipient of my wife's faith in action through the years, and it has motivated me to deny myself and love and cherish God's grace in my life.

Certainly, I realize that this is not a part of the spiritual curriculum nor the marriage curriculum that you thought you would have to take. It's not a course you ever thought you'd have to study for and pass—and yet here you are. Maybe you are in a situation where you were fortunate enough to have your spouse respectfully reveal their same-sex attractions and possible previous homosexual activities to you prior to marriage, giving you the much-needed time to think, pray, seek counsel and make appropriate decisions before you walked down the aisle (a better option, by far). Or perhaps this bombshell news was discovered or confessed to you once you were already wed (not the ideal option, but it doesn't have to be a game-changer either).

Whatever the case, I've got some really encouraging news for you: You can absolutely live in a happy, successful, faithful Christian marriage, even though the sexual orientation of one of you is toward the same gender. I want you to know that having a same-sex-attracted spouse is not a curse to the matrimonial union. Granted, it does bring its unique nuances and snags, but you can maneuver your way through them faithfully and lovingly—provided you focus on God and the biblical principles he has provided for us—and that is what this chapter is going to help you with. So, wherever you are in your relationship with a same-sex-attracted companion, I hope the following will be of some value to you.

If You're Dating and Are Ready to Escalate the Relationship

"I'm about to get engaged. Should I tell my girlfriend/boyfriend that I am same-sex attracted?"

I am asked this a lot, so let me begin with addressing those who are considering the idea of escalating their relationship from the status of "dating" to "engagement." There is only one answer to this question and it is an unequivocal, unambiguous, unmistakable, definite and explicit: "YES"! I cannot imagine a scenario where it would not be considered a wise move to reveal this information to the person whom you are about to ask to spend the rest of their earthly days with you. I've counseled couples where this was not done. Trust me, keeping your same-gender attractions secret from your spouse-to-be will only invite hurt, confusion and a deep sense of betrayal when they finally do find out—and they will most likely find out someday. It's not worth it, and it's not fair. I am not suggesting you do this in a new dating relationship, rather if you are sure you are ready to take things to a new level. In other words, if you're about to go ring shopping.

I will never forget when I spilled the news to Cathy. We had been dating for quite some time, and it was clear to both of us that we loved each other deeply and couldn't imagine being with anyone else. Needless to say, I was gobsmacked at this reality and unbelievably grateful to God for allowing this highly unlikely development to transpire in my life.

Of course, I also knew that if I was to really get down on one knee and pop the question, she would have to know that I had been involved in homosexuality at a different time in my life and was still attracted to the same sex. I'll admit that I was terrified to have this chat. Being homosexually attracted was very embarrassing to me and I felt quite a bit of shame about my sexual orientation and also shame from all of the homosexual activity I had participated in before becoming a disciple. I was also open to the fact that she might not want to marry me after having received this new information, and I had to be OK with that; it was a cost she would have to count. Being married to a homosexually attracted man could present several unique problems to her life, and she may not have been prepared for that.

Needless to say, I prayed fervently before speaking with her, asking God to help me trust his will in this matter—giving Cathy the freedom to choose how she wanted to live her life. I then asked a husband and wife in our church who had been long-time friends and trusted spiritual advisors to sit with us as I spilled the beans. I wanted to make sure that they were present so that not only could they help steer our conversation in spiritual, respectful and healthy ways, but also so that Cathy would have someone else to speak with besides me when our talk was done. I knew she would need the ability to talk openly, get advice and pray with a friend as she processed this new information. Our talk took no longer than thirty minutes. I did not go into details about my sexual past, and I would suggest that you do not either—beyond providing the general information that you were involved in homosexuality previously. If there are specific pertinent details that should be shared, the spiritual advisors you have chosen to walk alongside you in this will know you and your situation and can advise accordingly. I told Cathy that though I was still attracted to men, I had dedicated myself to God at baptism and not participated in any kind of homosexual activities since that day. I promised her that I never would again and that I was devoted to loving her and her alone for the rest of my days, should we in fact get married. I will say that being in a position to be able to share from a standpoint of strength and spiritual victory in this area (by that time, I had not acted out homosexually in over three years) certainly helped my cause. With almost twenty-two years of marriage behind us now, obviously she decided that I was worth the risk. Thank you, Jesus.

To summarize, if you are same-sex attracted and have been so blessed as to have found "the right one," and you are confident that you would like to see the relationship escalate to an engagement, in my estimation the following recipe for disclosure is the ideal way to go:

- Tell him or her about your sexual orientation and possible homosexual history before you ask them to commit to a lifetime with you.

- Do not get into details of your sordid sexual past, but do be honest about whether there is one.

- Make sure two mature and trusted spiritual advisors are present during this discussion and that your significant other is free to discuss this with them after the conversation has ended.

- Give your boyfriend or girlfriend the freedom to end the relationship if they wish.

- Share your God-centered commitment to purity and righteousness for the future.

- Pray that God will make his will known for both of your lives, and then faithfully trust the answer that the Lord provides through the answer that you receive from your boyfriend or girlfriend.

If you are surrendered to God about your life, then you will be submitted to his plan for your marriage and future relationship. Trust that he knows what is best for both of you.

Just as I wrote earlier in this chapter to the spouse or spouse-to-be of a same-sex-attracted person, I write to you here: This is an opportunity for spiritual growth if God is at the center. There has simply been no other element in my life that has spurred spiritual growth and maturity more than having to learn how to die to my sinful, selfish nature and to love and cherish this gift of God, my wife. What greater joy is there than being blessed with the prospect of learning to love like Jesus?

If You Are Married and Haven't Told Your Spouse About Your Same-Sex Attractions

I want to be careful not to offer a cart blanche statement and thereby paint every marriage with the same broad brush, for this situation is certainly not the same as a couple who has yet to be engaged, so my answer is not as unequivocal as the advice above. I will say what the ideal is, while recognizing that in some rare, unique situations, being open about your same-sex attractions to your spouse with years of marriage behind you may not be the wisest move. I personally think that such a situation would be extraordinary but not unmanageable. I strongly suggest you seek spiritual counsel if you think there is a legitimate—I stress again, legitimate—reason why you would not share this information with your spouse.

That being said, certainly the ideal is that if you are currently married but have not yet told your spouse of your same-sex attractions, you start planning on doing so. I'm not suggesting this be done immediately. Take time to pray and ask God to show you ways and what his timing is so that you can start coming into the light with your husband or wife. Ephesians 5:8–12 says, "For you were once darkness, but now you are light in the Lord. Live as children of light (for the fruit of the light consists in all goodness, righteousness and truth) and find out what pleases the Lord."

Disclosing this to your spouse would obviously need to be done with much prayer, guidance from trusted mentors and much sensitivity, thoughtfulness and grace. Husbands and wives who receive this kind of information after the wedding struggle greatly with trust, as they feel deeply betrayed and deceived, and the longer you've waited, the more difficult it will be for your husband or wife to hear this news.

You will need to give your spouse time to process this information, allowing them the freedom to ask any questions they wish as they go through this progression, having the liberty to seek advice from spiritual people in their lives. Do not chain them by saying, "You can't tell anyone else"; they will need counsel on how to proceed. That being said, they should not have the freedom to tell everyone they wish, as your confidentiality will need to be respected. Rather, the best scenario is that your husband or wife would choose one or two trusted, spiritual mentors who would respect your need for privacy as they offer their spiritual counsel.

With the above caveat already in place for those rare circumstances, please have the courage and conviction to bring this news into the light. Being transparent after the wedding will mean there will be some challenging moments ahead, but with prayer, forgiveness, spiritual guidance and a new commitment to righteousness and transparency, you will be able to get through this, and so will your spouse; many have, and you can too.

Five Practical Steps to Help You if Your Spouse Is Actively Involved in Homosexuality

If your husband or wife is involved in acting out homosexually, here are five practical steps that you should take to help both yourself and your spouse. These five points are from Ginger Haan, a wife and mother of two teenage boys, whose husband participated in several homosexual relationships over a period of eight years during their marriage but who ultimately repented and returned to his family. I have taken the liberty of adding my own thoughts for each of the five points that she presented in a class entitled "How to Develop Unconditional Love for Your Husband" at the 2007 Exodus International Conference in Irvine, California, which I personally attended.

1. Surrender your spouse to God.

Instead of spending your emotional and spiritual energies on trying to fix or heal your homosexually active spouse, I would suggest that you make the decision to surrender him or her to the Lord and focus your attention on your own spiritual well-being. God is taking care of your spouse—you need to take care of you. Trust that God is working on healing him or her of the emotional and relational deficits that brought about their sexual identity disorder and is maneuvering through their lives, working on bringing them back to him and to you. You must be patient, for it does take time.

Isaiah 30:20–21 provides us with a wonderfully comforting promise from God for those who are in the midst of adversity and confusion:

> Although the Lord gives you the bread of adversity and the water of affliction, your teachers will be hidden no more; with your own eyes you will see them. Whether you turn to the right or to the left, your ears will hear a voice behind you, saying, "This is the way; walk in it."

During the period of Judah's history when they were prosperous and comfortable, they paid little attention to God's voice and direction. But when there was "the bread of adversity and the water of affliction," they knew they needed God's guidance and help and were once again surrendered to him so that they were able to hear his voice. Likewise in your life, until you surrender, you won't hear God's voice. You'll hear your own.

2. Trust and obey.

When I meditated on the word "Guidance," I kept seeing "dance" at the end of the word. I remember reading that doing God's will is a lot like dancing.

When two people try to lead, nothing feels right. The movement doesn't flow with the music, and everything is quite uncomfortable and jerky.

When one person realizes that, and lets the other lead, both bodies begin to flow with the music.

One gives gentle cues, perhaps with a nudge to the back or by pressing lightly in one direction or another.

It's as if two become one body, moving beautifully. The dance takes surrender, willingness, and attentiveness from one person and gentle guidance and skill from the other.

My eyes drew back to the word "Guidance." When I saw "G" I thought of God, followed by "u" and "I." God, "u" and "I" dance. God, you and I dance.

As I lowered my head, I became willing to trust that I would get guidance about my life. Once again, I became willing to let God lead.

—Author unknown

I'm not a dancer. Dancing is much too complicated for me. Besides, at six foot four and almost three hundred pounds, I'd likely knock someone out as I tried performing some of my breakdance moves, so for the safety of everyone involved, I normally sit on the sidelines when the boogying begins. However, I do love the thought of learning to dance with God and letting him lead. Dancing with God means that you will trust him and obey him—even when you are hurt and confused and are unsure of the next move. It may be difficult to see today, but all of God's dreams for your life can still come true. They haven't died because your husband or wife is same-sex attracted, or even actively acting out homosexually. The question is: Will you allow God to lead you through this challenge in your life?

In Romans chapter 4 we are told of the powerful faith of Abraham, who had to wait twenty years for the promise of a son to be realized. Paul's narrative of that story beautifully crescendos in verses 18 to 22:

> Against all hope, Abraham in hope believed and so became the father of many nations, just as it had been said to him, "So shall your offspring be." Without weakening in his faith, he faced the fact that his body was as good as dead—since he was about a hundred years old—and that Sarah's womb was also dead. Yet he did not waver through unbelief regarding the promise of God, but was strengthened in his faith and gave glory to God, being fully persuaded that God had power to do what he had promised. This is why "it was credited to him as righteousness."

Because Abraham was only human, there must have been times in that twenty-year span when he questioned whether or not that was really the Lord from whom he had heard on that momentous day. He must have at times wondered if God might have forgotten about the promises he had once made. Yet through it all, Abraham's faith did not waver—even when the situation looked completely hopeless.

When you see your husband or wife struggle through life and your marriage is not what you had dreamed it would be, you may find yourself asking at times, "Lord, have you forgotten about me?" That's all right. The question for you is: Even when it seems against all hope that he or she will ever change or repent, will you fight to keep your faith strong and not waver through unbelief, being fully persuaded that God has the power to do what he has promised? Will you trust and obey and let the Lord lead you through this dance called life?

3. Have a vision for your marriage.

Helen Keller once said, "The only thing worse than being blind is having sight but no vision." If there has been infidelity in your marriage, it can be especially difficult to have a positive vision for the future. Pray that the Lord will give you vision—a dream for what your marriage can be while you trust and obey his leadings in your life.

Love requires patience, and we develop this through endurance. Endurance is the ability to withstand hardship and adversity. In Hebrews 12:2 we find two unlikely words that are put together in the same sentence, "cross" and "joy": "Jesus...who for the *joy* set before him endured the *cross*, scorning its shame, and sat down at the right hand of the throne of God" (emphasis added). Jesus was willing to endure the cross because he kept his inner vision of the joy of heaven. In your life and in your marriage you've got to keep believing and envisioning that something good is going to come from this so that you are willing to endure the difficult times.

In Romans 4:20–21 we see that Abraham gave glory to God even though he did not see the answer. His attitude was, "Lord, I'm going to praise you anyway." With this, Abraham was able to praise God before the answer came. You can do that in your marriage as well. Praise puts attention on God and not on your circumstances. Satan is always defeated when you praise God.

4. Carefully select your words.

When you are hurt, it is easy to want to strike back, and since most of us know that doing so physically is not a wise choice, the verbal attack often seems like a viable option. But we are called by God to use words and language that bring healing and not to use words that will add fuel to the fire. Proverbs 16:21 says, "The wise in heart are called discerning, and pleasant words promote instruction." Proverbs 16:24 says, "Pleasant words are a honeycomb, sweet to the soul and healing to the bones." Proverbs 20:5 says, "The purposes of a man's heart are deep waters, but a man of understanding draws them out." Our words have the power to build up or tear down, and as difficult as it might be—especially when you have been deeply wounded—you must ask yourself before you speak whether or not your motive is to bring about positive change, healing and spiritual dialogue. If so, your words will reflect your motives. If your intention is to be vengeful and cause hurt, your words will reflect that reality as well.

My wife, Cathy, stands as an incredible example of one who prays before she speaks to me about possibly contentious issues. There have been times when she has wanted to confront me about something or discuss an issue that was on her heart—including the topic of my same-sex attractions—but knew that if she did do so in the mindset that she was currently in, she would most definitely have a "toothpaste out of the tube" moment. Cathy has promoted healing and instruction in our marriage by sometimes taking hours or even days to first pray and then ask for direction and advice from trusted spiritual advisors, seeking guidance so that when she did eventually speak, it would be in the spirit of love, not of revenge. Her wisdom and discernment in this has helped our marriage tremendously.

5. Accept that the sins of your spouse's flesh are no worse than the sins of your heart.

As sinful as your spouse may have been in your marriage, you must take responsibility for the sins of your own heart. Matthew 7:1–2 very clearly speaks of our attitude of judgment and how we ourselves will fall under the same judgment that we use on others. I know that some of you reading this have been hurt incredibly because your spouse has been involved in sinful homosexual behavior. The Lord's heart breaks with yours for what you have suffered, and few will ever be able to appreciate the pain you have endured. However, he still expects you to forgive as Jesus forgave those who murdered him. That is the power of Christianity. Without that, what have we got but victimhood? Who wants to live like a wounded victim? The power of the cross says, "I will forgive you no matter what you've done to me. With the Lord, I have the power to stand up and choose how I will feel and respond, and I will not give over that control to anyone else but Christ." In this sense, forgiveness, clemency and compassion equals freedom—both for you, the one who has been so deeply aggrieved, and for your spouse.

Galatians 5:22–23 tells us plainly what the heart of God is like and how it is his desire that we live with these qualities: "But the fruit of the Spirit is love, joy, peace, patience, kindness, goodness, faithfulness, gentleness and self-control." There is no condition written that says, "Do this unless of course you have been sinned against by your husband or wife, in which case, this instruction is null and void." No, in fact, the very thing that makes these Spirit-filled qualities so formidable and beautiful is that we can live them out in our hearts and lives while in the midst of pain and not only in the absence of it. When you find yourself displaying the spirit of pride or self-pity or perhaps the unwillingness to forgive your spouse either outwardly or inwardly, ask God for forgiveness. Give those sins of the heart to the Lord and let God replace them with his fruits of the Spirit. For just as there are no insignificant cancer cells, all sins are deadly, and your iniquities of pride, arrogance, self-righteousness, judgment and lack of forgiveness will shipwreck your faith and destroy your soul. Remember who the enemy is: It is not your husband or wife; it is Satan.

Finally, when you pray for your same-sex-attracted spouse, know the difference between prayers of blessing and prayers of cursing. Praying over and over again the prayer that says, "God, please change my husband, make him repent" is really a prayer that says, "Lord, please change him or her so I can be happy." That is not the prayer of someone who has surrendered their spouse or their relationship to God. Pray for your spouse in a positive way, asking God to protect them and heal them; pray for spiritual restoration and for their soul to be saved.

A Note on Unique Spousal Situations

If you find that your husband or wife is spending too much unaccounted time away from the family, appears to have given up on this issue or shows constant disregard for your sexual health, or is blaming and exhibiting habitual patterns of lying; given the complexities and seriousness of the situation, you will need additional pastoral and professional long-term help. Of course, it is ideal when both individuals want to work on the marriage, but I do believe that if that is not the case, in extreme circumstances—such as those just mentioned—this is a time when a restorative separation with the purpose of reconciling the marriage should be considered. Let me reiterate that you seek much counsel from the spiritual leaders in your life and envelop the situation with prayer before any decisions are made.

However you do move forward, it is important to understand that the homosexuality that your spouse is dealing with predates the marriage; these challenges are not your fault, and you should never carry such a burden on your shoulders. Cling to God through this time; rest assured that he has you in the palm of his hand and cares for you beyond your understanding. He comforts those who mourn, and you may need to mourn a part of your relationship if you haven't already. Lean on him and get support from those you love and trust most. "Let the beloved of the Lord rest secure in him, for he shields him all day long, and the one the Lord loves rests between his shoulders" (Deuteronomy 33:12).

For Women Who Are Married to a Homosexually Attracted Christian Husband

For this section of the chapter, I thought it would be wisest to let Cathy speak about her experiences as a heterosexually attracted woman married to a homosexually attracted, faithful Christian man. Her words follow.

As a woman who is married to a man who is same-gender attracted, I am writing this to those of you also in this position to help you know that you are not alone and that what you are feeling and the questions you are asking are common to each spouse of a same-sex-attracted person. I also want to give you copious amounts of hope. My husband, Guy, and I have been married for almost twenty-two marvelous years, and while we do live with sexual identity issues as a reality in our marriage, it has not been a matter that has prevented us from being incredibly in love with each other and living a very fulfilled and happy life together. Regardless of what society tells you or what your fears and insecurities say, I want you to know that being married to someone who is attracted to the same sex is no deterrent to having a wonderful, love-filled marriage, provided that God is at the center of your relationship.

A few months before Guy asked me to marry him, he shared with me his past involvement in homosexuality throughout his teen years and even into his early twenties. He shared that he had been getting help, had repented, and had not been actively involved in this sin since becoming a Christian. There were several emotions and thoughts that came flooding in. My first reaction was that I felt like I had been kicked in the gut. I actually thought I might be sick. I felt so betrayed that I had been involved in such a trusting relationship with him while we dated and that I had even shared so much emotionally, but that he had hidden this huge secret about his life—what else hadn't he told me? I also felt so sad that he had gone through all of that, and I felt sorry for him because I could tell he was deeply ashamed. Mostly, though, I was proud of him for sharing this part of his life with me.

I went home that night and felt very conflicted. The questions that ran through my mind were overwhelming: Did he have AIDS? Had he been tested for it? Was he still attracted to other men? And if so, how could he possibly be attracted to me? And what of our physical relationship when we were eventually married? Would we ever be able to enjoy this? Could I ever really trust him, knowing he had hidden something from me for so long? Should I pursue this relationship and possibly end up in a marriage that could be a catastrophe? Could I trust God to lead me and take care of me in this? After receiving the assurances of the man who had spiritually mentored Guy during his time of repentance, I prayed and read scriptures about forgiveness and sin, and finally wrapped my mind and heart around the fact that before God, Guy's failings were no different from my own.

Over the last twenty-two years, we have had our challenging times. For years it was difficult for me to bring up questions or concerns because Guy would immediately get very insecure and withdrawn. He was still very ashamed and embarrassed about being same-sex attracted. The questions I had for years were: Are you still attracted to other men? Are you attracted to me? Are you attracted to other women? Are you afraid that people will find out about your past? In the last few years, though, our relationship has deepened in trust and communication. This has really allowed us to discuss these issues in a secure atmosphere, while we have faith in our love for each other and for God.

In one sense, Guy's issue with same-gender attractions has taught both of us to be incredibly sensitive to one another's needs. I have learned that my husband requires constant communication from me that he is attractive, that I am attracted to him, that I am proud to be his wife, that I am glad we are married, that I love him, that I am proud of him, and that he really does meet my emotional and physical needs. I realize that these are the same things every husband needs to hear from his wife, but Guy *really* needs to be reminded of this and hear these words of affirmation from me daily.

Most men live with a sense of feeling somewhat insecure at times, but same-gender-attracted men live with a very profound sense of insecurity. I know that Guy has those thoughts that say he may be less of a man because of his same-sex attractions, and those can be countered and even eliminated with my words of love, affection, admiration and trust. I have also seen that as he continues to find healing, the overwhelming sense of shame and insecurity that once plagued his life daily is slowly but surely being replaced with a strong confidence and healthy self-assurance in who he is as a male, a husband, a father and as a man of God.

Guy on the other hand has learned that I, too, need many of the same words of affirmation and warmth, especially considering his sexual identity issues. I need to hear often that he is attracted to me, that I satisfy him as a lover, that he needs me and that he's glad he is married to me. This is the kind of language with which we have tried to permeate our marriage. We are not perfect at it of course, but we really have spent years striving to constantly build each other up with words of encouragement, support and love.

I promise you that if you strive to love your same-gender-attracted Christian husband with the kind of love we read about in 1 Corinthians 13, your husband will cherish, treasure and protect you and respond in kind. In light of that kind of love, Guy and I have found that the sexual identity issues we must work through together (not to mention all of the other challenges that life brings) are actually quite small and even irrelevant.

What About Intimacy?

Many countries have a film-rating system in place to rate a movie's content suitability for certain audiences, thereby providing necessary warnings so that people (parents especially) can know in advance the age appropriateness of each film. Likewise, I want to offer a cautionary word regarding this section; it will not be suitable for all readers. However, I would be remiss to write a chapter specifically for husbands and wives who are in the midst of genuine perplexity in their relationship without addressing an area about which I am most often asked, that of physical intimacy between a husband and wife when one of the two are same-sex attracted. Now that a suitable warning has been issued, I shall press on.

Before Oprah Winfrey decided to go out while still on top of the television ratings and end her wildly popular daytime television talk show, she aired an episode on April 3, 2009 entitled "What Every Woman Wants." Since I'm a guy and don't have my PhD in this area yet, I gave Oprah Winfrey sixty minutes of my time. I'm glad I did, because it really crystallized what I had been learning these past two decades in my own marriage, what I've seen and heard in countless hours of couples counseling that I have been a part of as a minister, and much of what I've read in my own time of study and research. So kudos to Oprah for airing a show on this issue. But if I could be so bold as to add to Oprah's wisdom, I think that it is not just women who want this, it is men too! So what is it that every woman and man wants? Desire.

Dear wife, dear husband, if you are same-sex attracted, I know that there are some unique challenges here, but this portion of this chapter is filled with nothing but good news that will really help both you and your heterosexually attracted spouse.

What your husband wants from you almost more than anything else, except maybe respect, is to be desired. A lot of guys would want you to think that this is not true, that somehow it is not macho to want to be desired, but don't you believe it. Every husband wants to be desired by his wife.

What your wife wants from you more than anything else, more than financial security, more than a big house and a nice vehicle to drive, more than the occasional vacation and more than your incredible charm is to be desired and wanted. Don't get me wrong. I'm confident that financial security, a decent place to live, some nice trips and you being a spiritual maverick will all have their bonuses, and we as husbands need to do what we can to provide these things, but without you desiring and wanting her, you will have a hurting and disappointed woman on your hands.

The Unique Challenges We Face

I realize that I'm writing to a very unique audience: men and women who are married to the opposite sex, but who are at least in part or entirely sexually attracted to the same sex. I guess you could say we're in quite a predicament, aren't we? How can you show your love and affection to your spouse when you are attracted to the same sex? You may at first think that desire and sexual attraction are the same thing, but they are not. There is no doubt that they are closely linked, and for men and women whose sexual attraction is heterosexual in nature, they even overlap at times, but they are really two separate entities. That is tremendous news for the same-sex-attracted married Christian, and here's why:

Just because you are still learning and changing and growing in terms of being sexually attracted to your spouse does not mean that you can't desire him or her and in turn make your spouse feel desired while you and the Lord work together in developing this aspect of your relationship. And let me say here that this can absolutely happen; I am living proof. When I first married twenty-two years ago, I was fearful of how things would work out in this regard, but I can tell you confidently that over the years, it has been my experience that sexual desire for my wife has progressively awakened and increased and today I desire my wife sexually in a way I once would have told you was impossible. I truly only have eyes for her.

Regardless of where you are right now in terms of how sexually attracted you are to your husband or wife, know this: Your spouse wants to be wanted; that is key. And there is no reason why, even though you may be deficient as far as your opposite-sex attractions are concerned, you can't want your husband or wife at the same time!

I desire my wife for friendship, companionship and conversation. I desire my wife to laugh with me and to share my life's experiences with me, the good and the bad. I want my wife because my life would be so lonely and empty without her. I would rather talk to her than anyone. I would prefer go to a movie with her than any of the guys. I would rather watch a television show with her than anyone else. I would choose to go on a walk with her before any other person. I would rather have dinner with her than anyone else in the entire world. There is no one on the planet that I would choose other than Cathy to go on vacation with and spend my holidays and special moments with.

Do I love my wife? I do beyond words. Do I want my wife? You better believe I do! Do I desire her? Absolutely! The desire and longing for her and my unbelievable appreciation for all that she is for me make me want to find ways to show her how much I desire her and want her. How is this played out practically?

- I tell her all the time that I love her.

- I hug and kiss her every day, sometimes several times a day.

- I hold her hand.

- I put my arm around her.

- I plan special times together.

- I tell her several times a week that she is beautiful.

- When she gets dressed up to go to an event, I tell her how pretty she looks and assure her that she will be the most beautiful woman in the joint!

- When we're in bed, I hug her, hold her and tell her that I love her.

It is because I want her and desire her that I do these things, and the end result is that my wife feels wanted and desired—the very thing that she wants more than anything else.

Determine Your Own Success

I do not at all want to minimize the challenges that some of you are facing in regard to physical intimacy. I know that for some same-sex-attracted men and women, the actual act of intercourse with your spouse right now seems almost impossible for you. There is no need for you to panic or to feel inferior or like a failure. Nor is there any reason for a spouse to feel insecure or unloved because of a husband's or wife's present inability to perform sexually. It is not a commentary on how he or she feels about you. It is rather, simply one of the many ways that the complex and intricate realities of sexual identity disorder are sometimes exhibited, and it is also very common.

Couples that I have counseled in such situations have often discovered that by focusing their physical affection on times of cuddling, hugging and caressing, while verbally expressing their deep love for one another, rather than concentrating on the need to have intercourse—which often causes excessive and obstructive emotional pressure—will, over time (sometimes weeks, sometimes months), encourage a craving for escalated sexual activity. Remember, the ultimate goal is not sex; it is to desire, to show love, to display affection and appreciation and warmth and gentleness and tenderness. You can accomplish all of this even if you are same-sex attracted and currently have a difficult time expressing these sentiments physically.

Culture both inside and outside the church can often incorrectly dictate what is and what is not considered triumph when it comes to sexual activity in marriage. Couples can end up wrongly comparing themselves to what other married couples are able to achieve in this regard—both in terms of frequency and the type of sexual activity they involve themselves in—and somehow feel like they are failing if they are unable to enjoy the same measure of success as they hear others are enjoying. This is a mistake for husbands and wives who are dealing with such multifaceted issues as same-sex attractions in their relationships. In such cases, through honest and sensitive communication; through trial and error; with patience, kindness, warmth and thoughtfulness, and sometimes even through seeking advice from trusted advisors, couples should decide what their benchmark of achievement for them and them alone will be. Couples need to be able to define their own success and then celebrate and rejoice in one another and with God when they accomplish it.

Dear same-sex-attracted husband or wife, let the spouse that God has blessed you with be the desire of your life, and make sure he or she feels wanted. Do this by how you communicate every day. Express over and over again why you love and appreciate each other. Make sure this kind of dialogue is a normal part of your daily life. Stop and think about all the ways you desire your husband or wife, and think way beyond the boundaries of sex when doing so. When it comes to the intimate relationship that God has blessed you with, give yourself to your spouse. Work together with your husband or wife and define your own measure of success. And lastly, remember the day of your wedding, as it was your own special miracle that God performed just for you.

Resources

1. Connie Neal, *Holding On to Heaven While Your Marriage Is Going Through Hell* (Mun Gode Press, 2012).
2. Jim Burns, *Creating an Intimate Marriage* (Ada, MI: Bethany House Publishing, 2006).
3. Joe Dallas, *Restoring Marriages Damaged by Sexual Sin*, CD, www.joedallas.com.

Chapter Five

Practical Help for Parents

A mother who is really a mother is never free.

—Honoré de Balzac, French novelist, 1799–1850

Hello, I am sixteen years old. I have been a Christian for two years now. Prior to my commitment to Christ I was involved in some homosexual activity. Though this was confessed to my parents in the midst of my Bible studies, they believed it was just a phase that I was going through, but this is not true. I still battle with what you call "same-gender attractions." The man who studied the Bible with me told me that "gay people" get over their desires by practicing self-denial and loving Jesus. I heard this and started denying my reality and saying to myself over and over again that I am attracted to women, not men, but it did not work and I am still like this. But as far as everybody knows, I am attracted to women and all of the "homo" that was in me is gone. But as much as I want it to go away, it doesn't...I feel that I should tell some brothers in the church, and definitely my parents, but I'm scared. My parents have an extremely strong view on this topic, and from what they've discussed with me, I know what they think about it. I want to let them know, but I'm afraid because I want them to still love me, and I want them to know that I'm still a good boy...I just don't know how to just drop something like this on them. Can you please help my parents and me?

—A 16-year-old boy in the United States

I hate uncertainty. It's true that our lives and homes would be a lot simpler, and our churches a lot less messy, if all the issues we had to deal with could easily be categorized as being black or white, right or wrong, best or worst. But when it comes to the topic of sexual identity the issues are largely ambiguous. There is still a huge mystery factor when it comes to the causation of homosexual attraction. The truth is that you'll most likely never entirely know why your son or daughter is this way, meaning that anyone broaching this topic will need to learn to embrace mystery. We must somehow live in this land of not having all the answers and remedies while recognizing that this process could take a lifetime to figure out, and even that may not be long enough.

We all long for resolution. We want to arrive. We want the destination. And because the journey for both the same-sex-attracted child and their parent(s) is rife with hardship, sleepless nights, mental anguish and hours of prayer, we want to know that there is a meaning in this. Our desire for resolution is natural and understandable, but Jesus calls us to surrender our demand for resolution. More important than us getting the answers we want is the trust that God is simply asking us to place in him in the midst of paradox and mystery. While we want the answer, God is asking us to walk with him faithfully as we live in the midst of all this ambiguity, staying faithful and glorifying him with our lives. Of course, this is much easier said than done.

For you, the parent who only recently received the revelation that their child is attracted to the same gender and possibly involving him- or herself in homosexual behavior, you can feel as though a bomb has gone off in the middle of your home, your life, your plans. You are left trying to figure out how to put all the pieces back together again. You are most likely in a state of disbelief; you are confused; you are more than likely angry. For the parent who has been traveling down this road for a period of years and your child is now into adulthood, you are susceptible to growing weary—for you have prayed countless prayers and spent too many nights crying yourself to sleep. You may even be on the verge of losing faith in the possibility of change. It's so easy to lose hope when our world is so "gay affirming" and homosexuality is so celebrated—when God is so mocked. I hope that the following information and advice of this chapter will encourage you.

Recognizing these realties, I do understand that suggesting you embrace uncertainty may not seem helpful on the surface, but I am telling you that there is freedom in this. Not everything can be reduced to an explanation or a simple formula. To sit in the middle of this mystery and to say "I don't know" requires humility and surrender and ultimately, it takes faith.

Three Fundamental Truths

As someone who participated in homosexual activity from the tender age of twelve, all through my teen years and then into my mid-twenties, and yet who is today a faithful Christian man with a family; as one who has seen countless self-identified gay men and women return to their spiritual moorings and, like the biblical prodigal, come to their senses to live for Christ, I would ask you to remember three fundamental truths when it comes to your child:

1. Your child's spirituality is the primary issue.

The primary concern regarding your child's welfare is not their sexual identity; it is their spirituality. Your same-sex-attracted son or daughter can learn to overcome their challenges and live a Christ-filled, rewarding and happy Christian life. Same-sex-attracted disciples all over the world do this every single day. You, as a parent, can learn to be incredibly proud of that victorious child.

Speaking as a homosexually attracted Christian myself, I can attest to the fact that I would much, much rather live with same-gender attractions as a saved Christian who is going to heaven, than live as a heterosexual man who is lost and going to hell. Don't let yourself get caught up in the trap of allowing your child's sexual orientation to be the primary issue—it really isn't.

2. Your child is not inherently homosexual.

Your son or daughter is living a life that was not intended by God for them, although they may believe it is inherent in their nature to be same-sex attracted. It is not how God created them; it is not representative of how he ever intended for them to experience their sexuality or their relationships. Just like every living human being on the planet, your child is suffering the effects of living in a broken and fallen world.

That is good news for the parents of homosexually attracted kids, regardless of their age, because through Jesus, what has been damaged can be put back together again. There may be scars as proof that there was once an open wound, but the scars will also stand as proof that there has been healing. Such is the message of 1 Corinthians 6:9–11 when Paul addresses Christians, some of whom before becoming disciples were practicing homosexuals: "And that is what some of you were, but you were washed, you were sanctified, you were justified in the name of the Lord Jesus Christ and by the Spirit of our God" (v. 11). So, remain filled with hope—cling to it—for God is working to heal the wounds.

3. Your child belongs to the Lord.

The third fundamental truth is that God's call to your child is irrevocable: He will not quit calling them back to him. While biologically this is your child, spiritually he or she is the Lord's. To the divine, you are the surrogate mother or father, and the Lord is the true parent. He is continually, seamlessly maneuvering and carefully interweaving your child's world—whether you can see it or not—all in a constant effort to lovingly bring him or her back home to his loving embrace. Remember the comforting words of Hosea and let them warm your heart about how God feels about your child:

> It was I who taught Ephraim to walk,
>   taking them by the arms;
> but they did not realize
>   it was I who healed them.
> I led them with cords of human kindness,
>   with ties of love;
> I lifted the yoke from their neck
>   and bent down to feed them.
>
> Hosea 11:3–4

Three Necessary Steps

So with those three fundamental truths in place, let me offer three necessary steps that would be helpful for you to take in order to move forward faithfully:

1. Release yourself from blame.

What causes someone to be same-sex attracted? The bottom line is—no one can provide a definitive answer. There are many possible contributing influences to someone establishing a same-sex attraction. There is not concrete scientific research proving that there is a genetic or biological connection. We can, however, see the patterns over and over again that seem to point to contributing influences, and the list is extensive.

Whenever we are talking about any kind of human behavior, there is always the formula that involves the complicated combination of nature and nurture (My apologies to all psychologists for the embarrassingly simple definition that I am about to provide).

Nature has to do with biology, genetics and innate traits. Nurture has to do a with a person's experiences, relationships and environmental influences. All that is a part of the human experience (sexual identity included) intricately interweaves these two components of nature and nurture.

So let us start by looking at nature. What are we to determine about nature and the role it plays in the causation of homosexuality? Does it mean that there is a "gay gene"? No—not yet anyway, for one has not yet been discovered. It does mean that a child's genetic makeup influences or contributes to the complex dynamics that are occurring as they grow and develop and move through their sexual identity development. And while there may be no gay gene, nature does in fact play an indirect role in determining who we become.

As people strive to figure out why someone is homosexually attracted, they often look for someone to blame, and parents can be easy targets. This is mainly due to lack of education, myths thrown about in our culture and sometimes even the parent's self-inflicted guilt. We can become consumed with the need to find an answer; this is both unfortunate and unfair. From scientific study there is not conclusive evidence that genetics alone are responsible for same-sex attraction.

Now let's look at the nurture aspect. Remember, nurture has to do with a person's experiences, relationships and environmental influences.

I can tell you confidently that there is not one thing as a parent you could do that would guarantee your child will be same-sex attracted; in the same way, there is not one thing you as a parent could do that would guarantee your child will not be same-sex attracted. That is not to say that spending time investigating the familial dynamics in your home wouldn't be beneficial, but it is clearly only one part among many and is certainly not the proverbial silver bullet that many quickly rush to identify. You are definitely not the only influence in your child's life.

There is wisdom, though, in asking God where you have gone wrong in your parenting. As an imperfect parent of four teenagers myself, it is painful I know, but if the Holy Spirit reveals something to you, own it, ask for forgiveness and then don't look back. Press on toward the goal and forget what is behind (Philippians 3:12–13). If you have been carrying around a burden of guilt and shame—examining and reexamining, questioning over and over again where you went wrong in your parenting that caused your child's sexual identity confusion—it's time to let go of this line of reasoning and release yourself from a burden that you should not be carrying. If you have been blaming your spouse—accusing them of being primarily responsible for your child's sexual orientation—it's time to let go of this line of reasoning and release your spouse from a burden that they should not be carrying. I know that you're desperate to find an answer because you hope it will bring peace, but please realize that you are but a small piece of what has formed your child's life. There are just so many facets and contributing factors to your son's or daughter's homosexual attraction that are simply outside of your control. Nature and nurture both play a role in our development and neither is solely to blame for our outcome.

2. Relinquish your child to God.

If you haven't already, it is finally time to surrender your child to the Lord. This does not mean you abandon him or her, nor does it mean that you sit back and do nothing, but it does mean that in your heart and soul you resign your loved one to God. Unshackle yourself from the weight of responsibility that your child's standing with him and the future of his or her eternal destiny depends on you.

It does not. It will not. It never did.

Release your child into God's hands and let them work out their relationship. Humbly relinquishing your child to God like this will most likely be a decision that you will have to go back to and make several times as you move forward because, like all loving parents, you will often feel the temptation to try to grab that burden back. When you do feel that happening in your heart, let them go again. The burden of your child's salvation was never meant to be yours. To wisely teach, steer, guide and love is what all parents are charged with, but the rest is up to your child's own free will to choose how they will live their lives—and up to the Lord.

3. Respond with intention.

While you release yourself of blame and relinquish your child to the Lord, thereby allowing him to work his will on the spiritual side, how should you proceed in the physical realm as you engage your same-sex-attracted son or daughter? Respond with intention; do it on purpose. And make sure it's with a whole lot of determination, prayer, tenacity and resolve.

While Satan has tried to use homosexuality as a weapon of mass destruction in your family, you have to find within yourself the will and strength to fight back and not allow your family to be a casualty of war. Just because your child may be involved in homosexual behavior today does not mean that this has cemented his or her future, regardless of how old they are or how long they have been involved in homosexuality. All is not lost; there is hope, but you've got to learn to fight back against the devil and his schemes as he tries to kill off your family, and you must do so with discernment and shrewdness.

When dealing with your homosexual children, I suggest that you do not treat this as a "shock and awe" campaign where you as parents go to your kids with "all guns a-blazing." To win this battle for your family, you've got to treat it more like a "Special Ops" mission where you stealthily try to go in behind enemy lines and infiltrate Satan's territory to slowly but surely—over time and with much prayer and love—un-shackle your child from the chains of homosexuality and bring them back safely home. Remember, your child is not the enemy, Satan is the enemy; he has captured your son or daughter. Obviously, there is no option but to do something.

Will you do any of this perfectly? Of course not, but in the words of Theodore Roosevelt: "The best thing you can do is the right thing, the next best thing is the wrong thing, and the worst thing you can do is nothing." Often parents ask me what they should do or say when their child first comes out with the devastating information that they are attracted to the same gender or already involved in homosexual behavior. My answer is "engage"! In every other area of your child's life, since they were born, you have deliberately stepped in to protect your child if he or she was involved in any other kind of destructive behavior; there is no way you would sit back and do nothing, so do likewise with homosexuality.

You and your child may have taken a bullet or two and suffered some wounds in this war that Satan has initiated, but no one in your family needs to be a fatality. Let us go forward with this kind of fighting heart and attitude that says: "Satan may have started this fight, but the Lord and I are going to finish it—no matter how long it takes."

The Five Stages of Grief

In 1969 Swiss American psychiatrist Dr. Elisabeth Kübler-Ross published her pioneering book entitled *On Death and Dying*. In it, she discusses what is now known as the "Kübler-Ross model"—a theory based on her work with terminally ill patients in which she lays out the five stages of grief that one undergoes when they discover that they are soon going to die: denial, anger, bargaining, depression and acceptance. Of course, people who face far less foreboding ordeals than imminent death can undergo this five-stage grief cycle as well: the loss of a job or a home, divorce, and struggling through bankruptcy are some examples.

Certainly receiving the news that your child is homosexually attracted and is maybe participating in homosexual activity is another; the grief that a parent suffers is very real and powerful. I have heard parents say that when they discovered this information, it did indeed feel as if a part of them had died. Is that an overstatement? I don't think so.

A mother will grieve the loss of the dream of her child's wedding (at least the kind she had long envisioned) and most likely the eventual joy of her child having children, which means that there will be no grandchildren for her to love and cuddle. Fathers will grieve the loss of their child carrying on the family name. It is a true statement that finding out your child is same-sex-attracted and possibly homosexual is quite devastating, and all parents will go through the very same five stages of grief to one degree or another. Regardless of the point where you are in this process, it is important to respond to your child in a helpful, loving and respectful manner.

One thing that may be helpful to know: No matter how your world has been turned upside down, your child's intention was never to cause you any hurt or pain. By the time they have come to you to tell you their news, they would have spent much time in thought, in tears, in self-examination and probably in prayer. I know that revealing my same-sex attractions to my family was one of the most terrifying moments of my life, and I hear this same sentiment from same-gender-attracted disciples all the time. I take calls regularly from teens who wonder how they can share this information without hurting their parents or siblings. Letters like the one included at the beginning of this chapter are but one example of the kind of fear and confusion that same-sex-attracted kids go through when they want to tell their parents of their struggle:

> I want to let them know, but I'm afraid because I want them to still love me, and I want them to know that I'm still a good boy...I just don't know how to just drop something like this on them. Can you please help my parents and me?

Heartbreaking, isn't it?

Of course, there is little that can be done to lighten the initial blow, but I do hope you will find some peace in knowing that causing this kind of disruption in your life was never the intent. Your child loves you beyond words and is hoping you will feel the same way about them, even after they have shared so openly about this part of their lives.

Focus on Your Own Health

The Lord is just as concerned about your own spiritual well-being as he is about your child's. He is maneuvering and manipulating events in your life as well: He gently and lovingly nudges and tugs, trying to use these events to mature and grow you into the likeness of his Son. Your child is not the only one whom God is working on here. Why not allow this journey to be a powerful good, affecting positive growth in your life and for those in your family?

To be able to properly receive that kind of godly attention and move forward with intention and purpose in your child's life, you have to be healthy yourself, because you are most likely going to be in for a very long haul with your son or daughter. While you may be in a state of shock at first and even find yourself suffering spiritually because of this challenge, you do not have the freedom to allow that to be your reality long term. This is not a time to pull away from the Lord as Satan so desperately desires. I hate to state the obvious here, but if you've not been known as a prayer warrior in your Christian life, this is the time to start; and if you have been, this is not the time to stop.

Pray for yourself. Pray that you and your spouse would be closer than ever before and that you will work as a team to lead your family through this challenge. Pray that your other children will grow closer to God through this. Pray that God will use this area of challenge in your life to encourage and to help other families who are going through the same trials. If your son or daughter currently has a partner, pray for him or her too, for they are also a lost soul and one of Satan's casualties in this spiritual conflict.

Helpful Strategies to Use with Your Child

Often when I am speaking with parents of homosexually attracted children, I will ask them to tell me about their son or daughter, and I'll most often receive a description of a person who is: gifted, talented, intuitive, creative, kind, sensitive, a champion of the underdog, articulate and one who has many friends. Who wouldn't want to have their child described like this? Parents of same-sex-attracted teenagers, however, while using this kind of affirmative language when describing their kids, will often add that he or she is also very immature. Immaturity is just one sign that there are some developmental deficits, some issues that just never got completely finished in their childhood.

Because at its core homosexuality is a relational matter and not a sexual one, the underlying issues have much more to do with growth and development than anything else. In other words, something did not completely form at the rate it should have during their most formative years. For whatever reason (again, there are many contributing factors), your child did not experience all of the love, affirmation and validation for their true self and gender—either in the family or with friends, or even within themselves—and therefore grew up with gaps in their emotional growth and confusion around their identity. When this happens, it leaves the child searching for ways to fill those emotional holes.

Dr. Janelle Hallman is an internationally recognized expert in the area of female homosexuality and emotional dependency and the author of the book *The Heart of Female Same-Sex Attraction*, one that I highly recommend. At a lecture presented by Dr. Hallman, which I personally I attended, entitled "Practical Helps for Parents of Gay-Identified Kids" at the 2007 Exodus International Conference in California, she spoke extensively on the methods she uses when counseling parents of same-sex-attracted children. The strategies presented in the remainder of this chapter are credited to her work in this field and are coupled with my own thoughts based on my own personal experiences with this issue.

When the child becomes involved in a same-sex-affirming, nurturing relationship, it feels like it is meeting their developmental deficiencies. This becomes problematic because if there is still a legitimate need for parental or friendship-type nurturing, a sexual relationship can never provide what only mothers, fathers or a non-sexualized, healthy, same-gender friendship can. This is why gay men and women often move from relationship to relationship: because they are trying to get legitimate emotional needs met in a manner that will never be able to fill these holes. Can they get these developmental deficits adequately met later down the road in life? Yes, the good news is that everyone's development is fluid. The truth is, though, that there are methods that work and methods that don't work; homosexuality is a method that ultimately does not work because it will never fill those voids.

What can work is when a parent is able to provide an environment where the child can still acquire those missing developmental pieces later in life. By becoming one who is willing to work on skills and communication techniques that strengthen attachment with your child, it actually helps him or her in their process of formation, growth and healing. In doing so, you will be offering a quality of attachment and love that is therapeutic and assists in resolving some of these underlying emotional deficiencies that brought about the same-sex attractions in the first place. These are simple strategies that any parent can use over time that are proven to be very helpful. The goal of sharing them here is to help prevent your son or daughter from having the sense of being the identified patient or project of the family who needs to be "fixed," while at the same time keeping the dialogue open between you and your child.

Will using these or any other techniques "cure" your child of homoerotic attractions? Most likely not, for while there are some who claim to have achieved this kind of complete recovery (where homosexual attractions completely disappear and total heterosexual attractions are achieved), such cases are extremely rare. For most, the total elimination of same-sex attraction will not be realized on this side of heaven, regardless of what methods or therapies are employed. That, however, does not mean that we should not strive to encourage healing and completeness where we can for our children. In this sense, indeed, a parent who is really a parent is never free.

Dr. Hallman also offers the following steps that can strengthen your attachment with your child and help bring healing. This advice is very practical for any parent, though the language is specifically targeted at the parent of a same-gender-attracted child.

1. Focus on your child's gifts and talents.

Make a list of your child's gifts and talents. Make it as complete and as extensive as you can. When you become discouraged and overwhelmed, and at times this will be daily, refer to this list; read it over and appreciate all that God has blessed them with. This is important because, often in the midst of difficult and dark days, when hope seems far away, it can be easy to forget how wonderful this child of yours truly is. It will assist you in remembering that their same-sex attraction is just one small piece of their lives, not their complete identity, and that there is so much more to them that you love and that you can thank God for.

2. Use affirmation.

It is possible that children can grow up in a stable and loving home and not assimilate the affirmation that the parents attempted to provide over the years. It is also possible that in the midst of living busy and hectic lives we overlook the extension of words of affirmation for our children. It is also common that parenting styles have been passed on from generation to generation and offering words of affirmation on a regular basis has not been the kind of interchange that is a consistent part of your family dialogue. Whatever the case, as you intentionally move forward, regardless of your child's age—whether they are fourteen or forty—you need to find plenty of opportunities to shower them with words of affirmation.

When you observe them displaying qualities and traits of kindness and compassion, don't let those times slip by without commenting how much you love that part of them and how proud you are of them for it. You can do this even when your child is in a homosexual relationship and you witness how he or she shows compassion or kindness to their partner, for you are free to love your child for who they have become as a person, even when you don't approve of all of the decisions they have made for their lives. Don't be afraid to affirm the fact that your child is a giving and caring individual. That is a valid and a true part of their character, and representative of God's character. Let your child know that you've noticed the amazing qualities of their heart and that you are proud of the person they have become. If this kind of spoken support has not traditionally been a part of the dialogue in your relationships with your children, that's all right; the good news is that you can start today.

3. Don't attempt to explain to your child their homosexuality.

As a same-sex-attracted adult Christian man I have experienced much success in overcoming my homoerotic temptations, feelings and emotions, yet while I have had much victory over the years, it has taken countless hours of prayer and strategizing and discussion and confession and study and self-discipline, along with a total reliance on God, to achieve that success. It has taken grappling with myself, with Satan and with God. It has been the battle of my life. It has taken all I've got and then some more. To think that my forty-year struggle with same-sex attraction could be boiled down to a simple explanation and a bit of deductive reasoning would be offensive and also would signal to me that you are not appreciative of the fact that my sexual orientation is woven into my development as a man. It is not something that can be turned on or off at will or easily changed. If I could have easily figured out a way to change it by now, trust me, I would have.

Parents need to sit in the mystery with their same-sex-attracted children—especially if they are of adult age—and empathize with the complexity of their lives. I'm not saying that we should draw back from having deep conversations with our children on this subject or that we should discourage seeking for answers. If your son or daughter is at a place in life where they are willing to do this with you—that is amazing! What I am saying, though, is that we need to be careful not to offer simple and dogmatic explanations to such a complex issue.

4. Know your own history.

Do an assessment: Do you have intimacy issues, or have you suffered a pattern of broken attachments in your own past? It is quite possible that you may be lacking in some skills that can help you attach to your child or them to you. If you see in your own past, for instance, a history that includes abandonment, divorce, depression, mental illness, separation or even the death of your own parent-child relationships, chances are there is something in your own life that you may want to investigate so that you can connect with your own disappointments and losses. Be aware of your own story; this will help you attune to your child if he or she does perceive that they have suffered different types of abandonment in their own history. If you can connect with your own pain, you can more easily connect and empathize with your child's pain.

5. Have unconditional, radical acceptance.

Let me first define what I mean when I use the word "acceptance." Acceptance is not the same as approval, tolerance or the condoning of a behavior. You can accept and acknowledge in your own heart the current realities that your child is experiencing, without approving, tolerating or condoning their decisions or actions. Unconditional, radical acceptance is an attitude that says, "I will love my child, just the way they are. I will accept all aspects of their life, appreciating that they are broken and fallen in this sinful world, and I will love them to the best of my ability." Having this attitude is important because homosexuality is such a stigmatized issue. It could be easy to convey that we will withhold our acceptance of our child unless they are no longer sexually attracted to the same gender.

This is certainly not how Jesus thought of people. He was able to see men and women at their worst, and yet he accepted them to the point that he was willing to fellowship with these "sinners" and to love them. He obviously did not approve of the decisions and actions that these thieves, drunkards and prostitutes had made for their lives, but he did turn the religious world upside down by his desire to unconditionally accept them for who they were at that stage in their life; he genuinely loved and cared for them in spite of their extreme brokenness. His acceptance of them—his willingness to be with them, to dialogue with them, to eat with them, have fun with them—was not set on a sliding scale based on their righteousness or their willingness to repent or to even listen to his message. It is this same heart and attitude that we need to extend to our children when they are involved in behaviors that are not representative of what God wants.

As a parent, our goal needs to be to unconditionally accept who our children are and to love them, whether they ever change or not. You can absolutely be accepting, kind, gracious, tender, loving, fun, and a trusted friend and confidante to your child. One day, your child may view their homosexuality as sin and want to repent and give their lives over to the Lord and live by the Bible's standard on sexuality, or they may not. Don't pull back on your affection or what you used to do for and with them before you knew of their homosexuality. This is not approving of homosexuality; it is loving your son or daughter in the fashion of Jesus—and one of the primary ways for you to help unshackle your child from the chains of homosexuality.

Your goal in your day-to-day communication with your child is not to continually harp on why homosexuality is wrong, sinful and destructive. Remember, this is not a "shock and awe" campaign. I'm not suggesting that you stay silent about the biblical sexual ethic, but chances are that your adult child will already be well aware of the biblical view. If the general tone of your discourse is one of confrontation, opposition, correction or unwillingness to accept their current condition, your child will not be responsive and will most likely avoid speaking with you as much as they can.

Don't Focus on What You See

Finally, let me ask you to focus on what the Word says, not on what you see. Sometimes what you will see with your physical eyes is chaos and disorder—truly satanic qualities and hallmarks of homosexuality. As Christians, we need to be able to see with our spiritual eyes; this can only be done by concentrating on God's word and the truths that we find there. Claim and hold onto scriptures like Jeremiah 33:3 that says, "Call to me and I will answer you and tell you great and unsearchable things you do not know," Hebrews 11:1 that boldly claims a necessary declaration for every parent: "Now faith is being sure of what we hope for and certain of what we do not see," and 1 Peter 5:6–7 that says, "Humble yourselves, therefore, under God's mighty hand, that he may lift you up in due time. Cast all your anxiety on him because he cares for you."

Keep Offering Seeds of Reconciliation

Because this is a journey that could take years, pray that you can compliment your timing of intentional involvement with the Lord's timing. It may involve spending time together in an environment where the proverbial elephant in the room is invisible: where you and perhaps your entire family can engage in activities that bring back positive memories, or just be together where the "gay" topic doesn't come up. It might involve restraint on your part not to bring up the subject and to deny the urge to "understand" your child.

Regardless of what happens, keep offering seeds of reconciliation to your child. Your relationship with your children is precious. Value it as such and be determined to make it a place of reconciliation, not condemnation.

> Therefore, if anyone is in Christ, the new creation has come: The old has gone, the new is here! All this is from God, who reconciled us to himself through Christ and gave us the ministry of reconciliation: that God was reconciling the world to himself in Christ, not counting people's sins against them. And he has committed to us the message of reconciliation.
>
> 2 Corinthians 5:17–19 TNIV

There is a lot of good that can come from this: Your marriage can improve, your compassion for others who are weak and in the margins of life can expand, your walk with God can become deeper and more meaningful and your ability to counsel others can grow. Don't let your child's homosexuality be something that takes you farther from the Lord; let it be something that brings you closer. Don't let it tear your life down; use it as an opportunity to build it up.

Finally, it would do most parents a world of good to remember that their child is going to struggle with some area of brokenness in their lives. You may wish privately that it was not homosexuality, but the truth is, if it wasn't this, it was going to be something else. For a parent of a heterosexually attracted child to assume that because their child is not dealing with sexual identity issues they have somehow dodged a bullet would be wrong. If they have dodged a bullet on sexual identity issues, then you can be sure that another bullet has hit the bulls-eye. So, if you can learn to relax—remember, you have already relinquished your child to God—and be willing to accept that this is your life and that your son or daughter is homosexually attracted and most likely with a partner, you will be going a long way in creating an environment where there can be more discussion. You will be, no doubt, fostering an appreciation from your child that you love them and accept them, even though they are cognizant of the fact that you don't approve of what they are doing.

It is a fact that you cannot help change what you refuse to accept as reality. To keep communication flowing, it will be important to maintain a dialogue with yourself like, "I see my child right now for who they are telling me they are, because I want to connect with them." Have an attitude that says, "I will walk side by side, hand in hand with my son or daughter, even though we don't see eye to eye." Remember, your homosexual child is currently not a Christian, so don't expect them to live like one. Don't communicate an attitude that says you recognize that they are a sinner but will only accept them if they don't sin. God gives each of us the freedom to succeed and fail, and we need to offer the same freedom to our children.

As a parent and a fellow believer, I offer you this advice in love, with compassion for you and your child, in sincerity, in hope and in faith that God will move your heart and heal the hurt and pain that you may be experiencing. I believe with all of my heart that he is able to do immeasurably more than we can ever ask or imagine. It is my hope and prayer that as you move forward you would allow the Holy Spirit to guide your son's or daughter's life and that the decision to release yourself from blame would act as a fresh, spiritual breeze in your life. God is moving in that child's world, and he is moving in yours. Stand in awe of the miraculous ways that God is working and praise him for it. No one knows exactly what you are going through except God. However uncertain, however bleak, know that God is over all and through all and in all, and that he is the ultimate authority on all things. He loves your child more than you can even imagine.

Resources

1. Joseph Nicolosi and Linda Ames Nicolosi, *A Parent's Guide to Preventing Homosexuality* (Downers Grove, IL: InterVarsity Press, 2002).

2. Joe Dallas, *When Homosexuality Hits Your Home* (Eugene, OR: Harvest House, 2004).

3. Stanton L. Jones and Mark A. Yarhouse, *Homosexuality: The Use of Scientific Research in the Church's Moral Debate* (Downers Grove, IL: InterVarsity Press, 2000).

4. Janelle Hallman, *The Heart of Female Same-Sex Attraction: A Comprehensive Counseling Resource* (Downers Grove, IL: InterVarsity Press, 2008).

5. Anne Paulk, *Restoring Sexual Identity: Hope for Women* (Eugene, OR: Harvest House, 2003).

6. Mark A. Yarhouse and Lori A. Burkett, *Sexual Identity: A Guide to Living in the Time Between the Times* (New York: University Press of America, 2003).

Chapter Six

How to Share Your Faith with LGBTQ People

If you only have a hammer, you tend to see every problem as a nail.
—Abraham Maslow, American psychologist

I had no idea what I was getting myself into; I didn't ask many questions about whom the audience would consist of; I was just excited to have been asked to speak. My ministry was relatively new and mostly unknown, and except for a few invitations, up to that point I had not done much public speaking on the issue. So when the call came to travel to New Brunswick, New Jersey to lecture at Rutgers University on the topic of "Christianity and Homosexuality" on behalf of a church campus ministry there and a school organization called "Campus Advance," I quickly answered in the affirmative. What could go wrong? My assumption was that the audience would mostly be made up of friendly and welcoming Christian campus students eager to hear my story about how I had gone from being a homosexual to a Christian, along with some of my philosophies on helping others do the same. But that was not the main purpose behind the invitation at all, nor was the audience the kind I was expecting.

Instead of just wanting to hear my testimony (and why would you not want to do that?) this small Christian campus ministry of about twenty-five eager and enthusiastic students sought to use this highly controversial, hotly debated and divisive subject as an opportunity to reach out on their campus, as an evangelistic event. They hung posters and courageously invited as many people as they could, but once word got around, their upcoming event was not well received. I can understand why.

Only a few months before my arrival, the extremely antagonistic Westboro Baptist Church, an independent Baptist church from Kansas known for picketing at the funerals of U.S. servicemen, desecrating the American flag and carrying abhorrent and repulsive signs that read things such as "God hates you" and "God hates fags," had come to Rutgers University to hold their own event and to spew their ludicrous message.

Students and faculty of Rutgers came out in huge numbers to peacefully rally against this group, carrying their own signage of peace and love: sentiments that actually do embody the true Christian message. Good for them!

So by the time word got out on campus that a Christian evangelist from Canada was coming to speak on Christianity and homosexuality, the immediate assumption was that I would be coming with my own message of bigotry and hatred in the same manner that they had just experienced, which of course was the farthest thing from my heart, my mind and my message.

I'll never forget the call I received a week before I was to fly to Newark. The campus minister said, "I hope you've been having really good quiet times with God this week." Not being too confident of how spiritually significant they had actually been (it had been a difficult week), I sheepishly said, "Ah, they've been all right, I guess. Why?" "Well, because there are a lot of people upset that you're coming. Some students are going around the campus tearing down advertisements of the event. Word is getting around, and there are people who plan to attend and protest at your speech and even disrupt the meeting if needed."

Suddenly realizing that I was getting into something I had not planned for or experienced before, I quickly initiated a conversation on what kind of security would be needed for my safety; would the university police suffice, or would it be wise to ask the local New Brunswick police department to have an officer or two on hand? At the very least, I was hoping that one of the campus ministry guys would be some hulking bodybuilder who would easily intimidate any crazed attacker; maybe he could stand by my side? There was laughter in that call, but it was uneasy laughter on my end. What had I agreed to? Up to this point, my audiences had been made up of churches and church leadership groups. It was safe territory; I mean, even if you do a really bad job, Christians are just kind enough to tell you that you did great anyway and to thank you for coming. But at this event I was going to, from the sounds of it, I would be speaking to a large audience of mostly irate lesbian, gay, bisexual, transgendered and queer (LGBTQ) men and women and their supporters, who were angry that I was there and ready to let me know it.

It's amazing how quickly my personal quiet times with God suddenly improved! I did a lot of praying over the next week, asking God to give me wisdom and discernment and the proper bridge-building language that I would need to bring the true message of God and the biblical sexual ethic to this group of people in such a manner that they would actually want to listen to me.

I remember walking into the auditorium of 200 seats and meeting the approximately twenty to twenty-five Christian campus students hosting the event. How inspiring they were to me, how gutsy and faithful of them to do this. Was it possible for them to choose a more heated and contentious subject to tackle, especially on a university campus, I wondered?

The rest of the theater quickly filled up to capacity. As people entered, some with signs, some wearing T-shirts with rainbows and slogans promoting LGBTQ values, I thought it would be wise of me to be somewhat proactive and let people know from the start what kind of guy I am—a nice, friendly guy. One they wouldn't want to get mad at or protest against! So I worked the room—went from row to row—introducing myself and trying to shake people's hands, but most would have nothing to do with it. It was clear that my good looks and winsome personality were not going to be enough to warm the chill in that room.

Considering that I was speaking on the topic of homosexuality from the Christian perspective to an audience made up mostly of people who quite openly do not hold to that biblical worldview, I was vulnerable to a whole host of stereotypes and was positioned squarely against the cultural norms that most in the room celebrated. It was clear that this was going to be a tough evening. You could cut the tension in that room with a knife.

I gave two forty-minute speeches that night, with a time for Q and A afterwards. It was simply incredible to see how powerfully God worked that evening. When the time came for questions to be asked, I calmly, patiently, kindly and yet forthrightly answered them to the best of my ability. So many hands were raised for questions or comments it would have been impossible to get to them all. As it happens, I believe the Holy Spirit led me to choose the one hand that mattered most: that of a young woman who was part of a group called "LLEGO": the Lesbian, Gay, Bisexual, Transgendered, Queer, Questioning, Intersex and Ally People of Color Organization at Rutgers University. She stood and said that she and many in her group had come for a fight; that they had been preparing for days to argue with me, but after hearing the message I had that evening, there was nothing for her to say except that she had never heard of this kind of Christianity. She said that if this really was what Christianity was all about, even though she was not interested in becoming a Christian herself, it was a message that the whole world needed to hear. She then thanked me for coming and sat down. That was the last question I needed to answer. There was no fight, no argument, no disruption, no attack, no security needed. The night was done, and many of those who would not even shake my hand when they first arrived came and met me and shared their stories, and some even hugged me as they expressed their gratitude.

The Rutgers University campus newspaper *Daily Targum* reported on the event, and in that article, Shawanna James, copresident of the LLEGO group was quoted as saying, "It was good to get a different perspective I haven't heard about Christianity. I think it was great that a lot of people from the LGBT community came to hear this."[1]

The people I met that evening (at the end) were warm and kind and eager to have respectful dialogue. Their demeanor when they first arrived was not based on who they are as people, but on how they have been mistreated by many who call themselves "Christian" and who have not properly represented the loving message of Jesus. I left that evening with a deeper respect for these men and women. For many in the LGBTQ community, they believe Christianity is largely made up of bigots, homophobes and right wing conservative nut-jobs who are backwards and ignorant; sadly, some certainly fit that description. What I wanted them to know on this night was that beyond those few are true Christian men and women who genuinely care about the LGBTQ community and who are eager to have respectful discourse as they share the teachings of Jesus and the biblical sexual ethic.

The message that I offered that evening is what I want to share with you here as I give you my thoughts on how to share your faith and the good news of Christ with gay and lesbian individuals, some with whom you work, others with whom you go to school and some of whom are your neighbors and friends.

It Starts with Your Attitude

Before you open your mouth to speak, your heart, mind and sentiment need to harmonize with these following truths if the dialogue you are about to engage in is to be seasoned with salt (Colossians 4:6) and relevant:

1. Every person needs to be treated with dignity, kindness and respect, regardless of who they are attracted to, how they choose to live their lives or what they believe in regard to sexual expression and matters of faith.

2. The issue is about people, not sexual orientation.

All too often, whenever the church talks about homosexuality, it is in the context of something to oppose, but when the church talks about homosexuality it should be talked about in the context of people . . .

We need to see beyond gay, see beyond lesbian and see a person. We can act or come across, whether we intend to or not, as though sex or sexual attraction is the only defining factor in a human being. It is an important factor, but it's not someone's whole identity....Many Christians think they do not have any close personal relationships with gay people, and their perspectives and attitudes have been influenced by an interpersonal experience: things they've read or heard, or seen on television, or on the news. But behind the headlines, behind the faces on a screen, however, are the lives of real men, women and young people who navigate the reality of same-gender attraction in a society that makes it a constant uphill battle. Beyond the land of theoretical rhetoric and arguments and standing one's ground and political battles and choosing sides, lie real people, with real hurts and dreams and gifts and talents and families and careers and joys and sorrows and bills and exams and loves and lives.[2]

3. Many gay and lesbian people do want to know God. It is a misconception that all homosexuals are uninterested in matters of faith and the Bible.

4. Christians do not have all the answers on this topic. While God has clearly defined that homosexuality is sinful, beyond that reality, there is little that the Bible addresses on the topic. Besides some indirect references to homosexuality such as the story of Lot (Genesis 19, Jude 7, 2 Peter 2:6–7), the Bible actually only discusses homosexuality directly five times (Leviticus 18:22, 20:13, Romans 1:26–27, 1 Corinthians 6:9–10 and 1 Timothy 1:9–10) and certainly does not speak to causation. There are many, many contributing influences as to why someone is homosexually attracted, and neither the Bible nor science has given any definitive answers in this regard. About the only thing we know for sure is that no one chooses to be homosexually attracted. This means that you will need to speak with hesitancy when addressing this issue. This means that you will need to be honest both when you do have an answer available and when you don't. It means that you will need to be comfortable with the fact that much surrounding this topic is ambiguous. Understanding this will mean that when you do teach the biblical sexual ethic, it will be done boldly, yes, but also with compassion, sensitivity and kindness.

For some reason, we often seem to think that when we are talking to a same-sex-attracted individual about God, the first thing we need to tackle is their sexual orientation. Why? There is a whole person there that will need to be transformed into the likeness of Christ. This will be a process that will take time as the Holy Spirit moves in this person's life to bring them to conviction. Surely there must be other topics and issues you can cover and teach on besides their sexual attractions! Of course you will eventually get to what the Bible teaches regarding sex and relationships, but to go after this as a first priority and allow it to dominate the discussion would mean that your priorities are out of whack and that you're not seeing the big picture in this person's life or God's will for them.

If you can converse understanding these realities, you'll be going a long way in being able to speak the truth in love.

The Goal Is to Keep the Conversation Going

Typically, when a Christian comes into contact with someone from the LGBTQ community or a supporter of gay rights, the first question that is put to the Bible believer is something close to this: "What do you, or what does your church believe about homosexuality?" It's at this point, right at the beginning of the dialogue, that things often quickly go awry and the conversation hits a major roadblock because the Christian most often replies with something that resembles this answer: "The bible teaches that homosexuality is a sin." End of discussion.

Given that response, we must ask ourselves: Why would the inquirer want to continue investigating the Christian's viewpoints on this issue, since a definitive, conclusive and final response has already been provided? There would be no need for further discussion; the response would have closed any need for it.

It's not that homosexuality is not a sin; the response provided is quite correct—homosexuality is a sin. But we must ask ourselves: Is it possible that there are times when the method in which the answer is given is almost as important as the answer itself? If the response shuts down any further dialogue, how will one be able to share the good news of Jesus? In giving the response that homosexuality is a sin, they certainly would have offered a biblical truth, but surely there is more than that immutable fact that God would want shared.

An Example from Home

If one of my teenagers were to ask me how I felt about him or her becoming sexually involved with a girl or boy at school (Lord, help me!), I suppose my first reply could be, "Don't you dare; the Bible says it's a sin, and if you do, you will be grounded until you're fifty!" But allowing this to be my first response would be shallow and shortsighted, in my estimation. While the answer would indeed be correct, offering such a categorical retort would most likely close any possibility for further dialogue with my child. Wouldn't it be wiser to begin a conversation that attempted to draw out important information like: Why does my child feel this need to become sexually active with either sex; what recent events might have occurred in their life for them to consider this kind of decision; what emotional needs are they trying to meet by becoming sexually active; and have they considered the enormous life-altering consequences of this kind of decision?

Being able to uncover this background information would require me to encourage openness and transparency through dialogue, asking exploratory and open ended questions and even showing an appreciation on my end that I understood why they would want to be involved in a sexual relationship. In fact, it would provide me with the unique opportunity to share that I was sexually involved as a teenager and that I have been paying the consequences of that decision for decades. Been there, done that; it's not worth it.

Keeping the conversation going with my child would allow me to tell them how Satan operates by luring us with activities that seem fun and exciting at first but that are in fact a snare that will cause massive amounts of hurt, guilt and shame afterwards. It would permit me to truly share my faith with my child by telling him or her that as exciting as sexual activity may seem to them now, if they can just wait and do it in God's timing—when they are married, as the Lord has planned— they will enjoy the blessings of that decision for the rest of their lives. It would permit me to then tell them that because I can't police their lives 24/7 like I could when they were younger, I know that this will be a decision that they, and they alone, will ultimately have to make for themselves; and while I beg them to take seriously my heartfelt words of caution and what the Bible teaches on the subject, if they do in fact decide to be sexually active, I will be there for them when they realize they have indeed been ensnared, and more important, so will the Lord.

This kind of dialogue will let me tell my child that no matter what they do in life, I will be there for them, that I will never think less of them regardless of what they do, and that no matter what occurs in the future when they are in trouble, we'll get through it together with God's help. This kind of conversation will permit me time to pray with my child, asking our heavenly Father to give my son or daughter the courage and strength and wisdom they need so that they can stand up against the prevailing forces of Satan and the cultural norms in which they live.

Don't you think that would be a better way to respond than to simply say, "No, it's a sin"?

Proverbs 20:5 says, "The purposes of a man's heart are deep waters, but a man of understanding draws them out." There is no "drawing out" involved when we use our words to shut down discussion, even if the answer is correct!

Considering this, what response could Christians provide that would encourage further discourse, not discourage it, when speaking on the issue of homosexuality? What answer could they produce that would offer time and room to speak to the very essence of the gospel, instead of sabotaging the discussion so quickly with a quick retort that leaves no opportunity to speak Jesus into the person's life?

Paul in Athens

In Acts chapter 17, in order to protect Paul from Jews who were following him from city to city stirring up trouble, the apostle was secretly whisked away to Athens where he waited for Timothy and Silas to join him. While he waited, Paul did what any of us would do today were we to go to Athens, Greece: He played tourist and explored the city. As he saw the sights, Scripture tells us that he became greatly distressed over the sheer number of statues and idols that populated every part of the capital, all of which were "related to the worship of the Greek pantheon, and its culture was pagan. Therefore Paul, with his Jewish abhorrence of idolatry, could not but find the culture of Athens spiritually repulsive."[3]

How did Paul handle himself in this situation? He certainly could have started his speech by saying, "Men of Athens, I can see that you are wicked and sinful for you worship idols. If you don't repent and turn to Jesus, you will all be doomed to hell." It's not that Paul would have been factually incorrect in saying this, but he does show us that just because you have the truth doesn't mean that you have to hammer people over the head with it at the first possible opportunity! In fact, continuing in the "hammer" theme, as Abraham Maslow, the famous American psychologist, so brilliantly once said, "If you only have a hammer, you tend to see every problem as a nail." I'm sure Dr. Maslow was not referring to ways that Christians can effectively share their faith when he offered this sage wisdom, but that analogy can easily describe many Christians and their approach to teaching people about the good news of Jesus, especially when it comes to this topic of how to engage individuals on the issues of sexual expression and faith.

I think it would be helpful to pause and consider just how severely Paul would have been repulsed by this idolatry that he witnessed as he strolled the streets of Athens. Yet when he had his opportunity to challenge it, we see him not only keeping his emotions and words under control, but also actually going out of his way to find common ground with these people with whom he so completely and utterly disagreed. By finding an altar with the inscription: "To An Unknown God," Paul was now able to use that as an opening, an opportunity to explain to them that this "unknown God" was the one, true and only God, who raised Jesus Christ from the dead (vv. 22–31).

By using this strategic and thoughtful method of evangelism, Paul now was granted more time to speak. In this way, he succeeded in keeping the conversation going (vv. 32–34). He even converted individuals to Christ after preaching in that city, many of whom would not have become disciples had he started with the "repent or perish" hammer at the very beginning of the lesson.

What Paul literally did was begin the conversation by acknowledging what the Athenians valued, and then he slowly and methodically taught them what he valued. All too often, Christians expect people to begin the conversation at a common point of understanding, but such an expectation is unfair and unrealistic. Does it not make more sense to imitate Paul's approach by starting the dialogue by acknowledging where our hearers are at, and then systematically and logically bringing them to a place of biblical conviction?

Paul's approach was not an accident. It was well thought out, and we would do well to replicate his methods as we stroll through our cities and experience the same distress that he did when we see people worship their own forms of idolatry, in this case, homosexuality.

Finding a Place of Common Ground

What common ground is there then, between one who believes in the biblical worldview and who is heterosexual, and one who does not believe in the biblical sexual ethic and who is homosexual?

In an earlier chapter ("How Homosexuality Deceived Me") I discussed how the vast majority of us enjoy drinking soda products, even though study after study continues to prove that drinking these carbonated concoctions of syrups and chemicals is incredibly unhealthy for our bodies. The fact is that none of us needed to read a study to recognize this reality. All one has to do is read the side of the can to know that these drinks are not healthy for us to consume, at least on a regular basis. So why do we keep drinking the stuff? Because they taste great; because on a hot summer day, few things taste better than an ice-cold soda. The trouble with these products, however, is that they quench our thirst for only a short period of time; it doesn't take long before we are left thirsty again. Only clear, clean drinking water can quench our physical thirst in a way that is healthy, fulfilling and long lasting.

This is the same way that sin works. It tastes great, it satisfies a legitimate need, it makes us feel better—but only fleetingly. All sin can offer is a short-term satisfaction with no long-term fulfillment. In fact, when it comes to iniquity, we are always left more emotionally thirsty than before we engaged in the sinful activity to begin with.

In my own experience this was how homosexuality worked. There were few things that I turned to in order to quench my emotional thirsts more than to homosexuality. From my youth, whenever I felt alone or insecure or afraid or unloved or insignificant, I learned to turn to homosexual behavior to meet those very genuine needs. And it worked. Participating in those homosexual relationships and activities did leave me feeling satisfied, loved, cared for, accepted and important. After a short period of time, however, I was always left feeling even thirstier emotionally, satisfied momentarily but never truly fulfilled. The problem was that I knew of no other viable option to turn to that would really quench my thirst long term.

Like the woman at the well in John chapter 4, when I discovered that Jesus was offering life-giving water that would take care of my very legitimate emotional needs in a way that would quench these desires forever and in a manner that homosexuality never could, following Jesus became the smartest option to take.

The common ground, therefore, is found in the fact that we are all guilty of drinking from the wrong well in order to get our emotional needs met. You may never have struggled with homosexuality, but absolutely every single one of us has spent ourselves on sinful activities that might have satisfied us momentarily but that ultimately only left us wanting for more when we were done. In this sense, sin has lied to each of us; we've all been had, and we all are guilty of buying counterfeit goods: sin that promised so much but delivered so little.

Therefore the broken human condition in this fallen world is our common ground. Having lived the very human experience of choosing to sin in order to enjoy momentary satisfaction, only to suffer the letdown when we are left unfulfilled, is a worldwide collective experience that each and every one of us can relate to.

A Possible New Response

So when a Christian comes into contact with someone from the LGBTQ community or a supporter of gay rights, and the inevitable question is eventually asked "What do you believe about homosexuality?" there is a possible response I want to offer that I believe could assist in finding the necessary common ground, thereby giving the Christian the opportunity to keep the conversation going so that they can eventually share the good news of Jesus, just as Paul did when he taught in Athens.

Instead of saying, "Homosexuality is sinful," the response I am suggesting is the following: "I understand why people are involved in homosexual relationships. I think homosexuality meets a lot of very legitimate needs in peoples' lives. I get it. But I also believe there is another option available that will fulfill a person in a much more complete and thorough way than homosexuality or anything else ever could, and that is in following Jesus. As beneficial as homosexuality may seem, Jesus is so much better. The reason why so many do not follow him is not because what he offers is lacking, but rather because people just don't know the real Christ. If people actually knew how marvelous, how loving, how forgiving, how compassionate and how totally rewarding and fulfilling Jesus is when it comes to meeting our emotional deficits and the empty parts of our hearts, everyone would want to be a Christian. The problem isn't Jesus, the problem is that most people just don't really know him yet! That is the Jesus that I want to tell you about."

Dear Christian, I believe that if you can find your own terminology to express the above sentiment, it will propel further discussion, not kill it. For you would have found common ground in expressing an appreciation for why people would turn to homosexuality, while letting them know that there is a much better option available in Jesus. And while many will immediately think they already know all about Christ based on past experiences, you will be telling them that there is so much more to learn and that you would like to continue to discuss it with them. You will then be free to continue your dialogue, inviting them to church or to a local Bible discussion group, or even to a personal one-on-one Bible study where you can teach them about our remarkable and wonderful Lord.

The Greatest Sales Job in the History of the World

Every day we are faced with multiple choices between products that advertisers claim can do so much for us. Let's take laundry detergent as an example: The grocery store near my home has devoted an incredibly long aisle to a seemingly endless number of soapy choices, all asserting that their cleanser is the one special detergent that can take the stains out of my clothes better than any other detergent. Even though each brand really does almost the same quality work, they all try to convince me that their secret and superior formula of soap and water will do what no one else's mixture of soap and water possibly can. I'm sure the truth is that they all work fine. I mean, how hard is it to screw up soap and water, right? Normally, when presented with so many detergent products to choose from, people will find a brand they like and then stick with that based on price point and, well in my case, smell. Personally, I like my clothes to smell lemony fresh. I don't want them smelling like lavender. So we stick with a brand based on that incredibly technical and important criterion.

But let's suppose that one day I actually found a detergent that really did take out stains better than anything else we had ever experienced, and smelled more lemony. Provided that the price point was right, I can promise you we would change brands. I mean, who would continue to buy an inferior product once they were convinced that there was another product available that worked much better? They wouldn't.

Not that I want to reduce Jesus down to being a product, but in today's world where Satan has provided so many choices for people when it comes to giving their hearts, it seems Jesus has become just one of thousands of options, all promising to provide satisfaction and fulfillment. As people stroll down the aisle of life to see all that is being offered, Christians have to be able to convince the world that Christ is the superior product: that he can take out stains better than anything else they could possibly try! In one sense, it is the greatest sales job in the history of the world because eternal consequences are at stake.

I believe that if we can individually be open to improving our "sales pitch" as we present Jesus to this lost and dying world, if we will be willing to attempt new methods and investigate what different strategies might work in today's context, and in doing so improve our ability to explain to people why Jesus is indeed the far superior product to anything else on the market, then people will be willing to switch brands—in this case, from homosexuality to Jesus. Christ will have become the better choice.

A Word About Friendship

> Many Christians think they have only two options when it comes to teaching about their faith: the "repent or perish" approach, or tolerance. But I would suggest there is a third option that most Christians don't consider, or if they do, have little time for: and that is hospitality.
>
> Hospitality creates a space to welcome the guest; it creates room and time for people to explore differences. The Christian community, when it is living consistently in the way of Jesus, is to be marked by a spirit of hospitality: acknowledging difference, teaching biblical truth, but still extending a welcome while people learn and question and try to figure things out. In a pluralistic context, extending such hospitality is a way forward in the midst of diversity.[4]

The Christian's fear is that leaving space for hospitality will mean that they are lowering biblical standards and appearing to approve of behaviors with which they do not agree. But there is a difference between *acceptance* and *approval*. The whole beauty of Jesus was that his acceptance of people was not conditional on his approval.

A Word on Bullying

It's quite a nondescript little building. When I first saw it in person, I was struck by the dullness of its façade. On the inside it's not much to speak of, either; one would never know that what transpired here decades ago ignited a firestorm of riots, protests and a movement that has transformed the world in which we live, from the laws of our countries (most especially throughout North America) to what our children are taught in school, to what we watch on television. The Stonewall Inn, a gay bar in New York City and the site of the infamous "Stonewall riots" of 1969, stands as the heart and starting place of what we know today as the Gay Rights Movement.

In the early morning hours of June 28 of that year, police raided the business yet again, something that had become quite a common event. This time, however, they were accused of brutality, and if you were to read the many reports of what occurred during that early morning raid, you would have to agree that the authorities were indeed cruel in their treatment of those who were there. Scuffles turned to fights and fights to riots, and riots to long-term protest, so long term in fact, that we still see the effects of the infamous "Stonewall riots" of 1969.

Gay men and women have often suffered verbal, emotional and physical abuse. As Christians, I believe that we need to stand with our gay friends and neighbors when we witness this occurring. This is an opportunity for Christians to show this community and the world that although we may not see eye to eye on the issue of homosexuality and how it relates to matters of faith, when it comes to ill-treatment and cruelty of any kind, followers of Jesus will stand side by side with the mistreated.

When a follower of Christ witnesses people making jokes at the expense of others at school or at work, or worse, observes someone being physically manhandled because of their sexual orientation, we need to stand up for those who are being mocked and ridiculed and not be afraid of stepping in to protect those who are being mistreated. When we hear of groups like the Westboro Baptist church spewing their message of hatred, true Christians need to be vocal in our support of gay men and women.

Those whom I met at Rutgers University that night had wrongly stereotyped me for who they thought I would be, based on the badge that

I carried that said "Christian." It took time for them to hear my message and what Christianity truly is in order for them to be willing to converse with me. Likewise, we can sometimes wrongly stereotype those in the gay community, making wrong assumptions about them and their lives based on the badge that they carry that says "homosexual." I believe that if we but focus not on these titles and names, but on people, offering respect even though we disagree and then considerately and humbly discussing the issues at hand while we focus on building relationships through offering hospitality, we will be well on our way to being able to truly bridge this huge space that often separates us.

Resources

1. Chad W. Thompson, *Loving Homosexuals As Jesus Would: A Fresh Christian Approach* (Ada, MI: Brazos Press, 2002).
2. Alan Chambers, *Leaving Homosexuality: A Practical Guide for Men and Women Looking for a Way Out* (Eugene, OR: Harvest House, 2011).
3. *Bridging the Gap: Conversations on Befriending Our Gay Neighbours*, DVD (Toronto, Canada: New Direction for Life Ministries, 2009).

Chapter Six Endnotes

1. Dennis Comella, "Gay Minister Preaches Tolerance in Church," *The Daily Targum* (Rutgers University, New Brunswick, NJ), March 8, 2010.

2. Wendy Gritter, *Bridging the Gap*, CD (Toronto, Canada: New Direction for Life Ministries and Bridgeway Foundation, 2009).

3. Kenneth L. Barker and John R. Kohlenberger, *Zondervan NIV Bible Commentary*, vol. 2 (Grand Rapids, MI: Zondervan Publishing House, 1994), 476.

4. Wendy Gritter, *Bridging the Gap*, CD (Toronto, Canada: New Direction Ministries and Bridgeway Foundation, 2009).

Chapter Seven

Answering the Most Often Asked Questions About Homosexuality

Maneuvering through these issues as a Christian is difficult to say the least, so permit me the right to begin this discussion with a few disclaimers. First, I do not have all the answers. As I have stressed elsewhere in this book, I have questions myself that remain unanswered, and I have had to be willing to live with the tension of uncertainty on the issues of sexual expression and how it merges with Christian doctrine and faith.

I also realize that my position on some of these topics is going to draw some fire, as not everyone reading this will agree with my standpoints, and that is fine. These are confusing issues, so it is good that we are addressing them together, trying to find ways to best communicate the message of Jesus to the lost and learning how to be more compassionate and understanding toward the same-sex-attracted disciples in our churches.

Is there a genetic cause for homosexuality?

What causes homosexuality? The truth is, no one knows. I have addressed the genetic argument in more detail in an earlier chapter entitled "Practical Help for Parents" and would suggest you read it if you haven't yet. There is certainly a wealth of information available for those who desire to study this in greater detail than what I am offering here. One tremendously helpful resource is a book entitled *Homosexuality: The Use of Scientific Research in the Church's Moral Debate* by Stanton L. Jones and Mark A. Yarhouse.

For the purpose of this section, I want to offer a quote from Exodus International, the world's largest multidenominational Christian organization dedicated to helping those who live with unwanted same-sex attractions.

> Genetic linkage and association are not equivalent to genetic causation. Even so, numerous studies analyzing a potential "gay gene" have been conducted over the last fifty years, but none have been replicated to conclusively prove that homosexuality is determined by genetics alone. In addition, researchers have not found a 100% correlation among identical twin studies in their study groups; if homosexuality is solely a genetically based trait, there would obviously be no variance among identical twins that share the same genetic history.[1]

Even The American Psychological Association, a group known for its pro-gay leanings, and who in the early 1990s stated that there was evidence to suggest that biology, including genetic or inborn hormonal factors, played a significant role in a person's sexuality, officially changed that view in 2009. Their position now reads:

> Although much research has examined the possible genetic, hormonal, developmental, social, and cultural influences on sexual orientation, no findings have emerged that permit scientists to conclude that sexual orientation is determined by any particular factor or factors.[2]

The bottom line on this question is that science has yet to prove that there is a genetic cause for homosexuality, and the Bible does not provide an answer to this either, except to speak to the reality that we are all born into a broken and sinful world, and all of us display our areas of brokenness in many different forms.

However, even though there is no scientific proof of a genetic cause, I can tell you as a same-sex-attracted Christian that I fully understand why people argue that they were "born this way." Why? I never woke up one morning and simply decided to be attracted to the same sex. It's all I've ever known, and I would have gladly given my right arm and more to have it taken away.

As a Christian, however, it really doesn't matter whether genetics are involved or not. I know that nothing gives me the right to sin. So, even if I *was* born with same-gender attraction, Jesus calls me to live for him and to not allow myself to be mastered by these temptations (1 Corinthians 6:12). It is my cross to carry in order to be a disciple of his, and it has been a cross that I have been more than willing and eager to carry for almost three decades because I love Jesus and want to honor him with my life (Luke 14:27).

There is a common thought in our culture today that says, "If it feels right, do it, as long as you're not hurting anyone else." This line of reasoning certainly is often conveyed when it comes to those who identify themselves as gay. The disciple of Jesus cannot allow himself to consider such opinions possible for their own lives. Clearly, that line of reasoning does not work in any other example of temptation.

For instance, the Bible is clear about the fact that lying is sinful. Whether one is genetically wired to be deceitful or not is not worthy of consideration, for nowhere in Scripture does it say, "Thou shalt not lie, unless of course you are genetically inclined to be deceitful, in which case you get a pass on this commandment; go ahead and lie your way through life."

Am I born homosexual? No; or at least, no proof of this has yet been discovered. Am I born with the predilection to sin? Yes, but my goal is to live righteously. For the same-sex-attracted follower of Jesus, the ultimate goal is not to achieve heterosexuality, but to strive to be holy. As for how to handle this discussion when it arises with someone who does argue that people are innately born with same-sex attractions, I would suggest you not make it a point of argument. The reality is that because no immutable evidence has ever been provided that confirms that people are "born this way," regardless of what Lady GaGa says, it's simply an opinion. In order for this assertion to become a legitimate argument, it must first be reinforced with actual substantiation. It's not your responsibility to provide evidence that people are not born homosexual; the burden of proof lies with those who make the claim that they are. In a respectful manner, ask people to provide what evidence they can put forward (beyond emotional reasoning) that confirms that this is a reality, in order to back up their claim. If they are able to provide evidence that they believe is applicable, you will then be able to continue with the dialogue.

Should a same-sex-attracted Christian make their struggle public?

Every person holds exclusive rights to their story; it is their personal information; it's like copyrighted material. No one should ever feel pressured to let their same-sex attraction issues be known publicly. Every individual should have the right to disclose this information to whom they wish and in the timing that they desire.

There is a difference, however, between releasing this information publicly and releasing it privately. I do believe that it would benefit every disciple of Christ to have at least one or two trusted and spiritually mature confidantes with whom this information could be shared. It has been my experience that without total and complete transparency with these types of men in my life, I never would have experienced the kind of victory over my sinful nature that I have experienced.

I will also say that should the day come when you feel the desire to "go public," as I have, with this private information because you long to help others, there are some things of which you need to be cognizant:

- You should not do this until you have spoken to your immediate family first and even received their permission to move forward. Your struggle with same-sex attractions should never be the type of thing your spouse or children would hear of for the first time as you stand up in front of an audience to share your testimony.

- If you are going to write an article or book that will be in the public eye, you will need to first make sure that other important family members (Christian and non-Christian alike) such as your parents and siblings are aware of your homoerotic attractions. Again, this is not something they should find out about for the first time as they read an article on the Internet.

- Do not share this information unless you can clearly and unequivocally do so from a standpoint of strength and a history of personal righteousness; in other words, your homosexual attractions do not have control over you, but you have control over them; this needs to have been proven by how you have lived your life. In my estimation, if you have been acting out sexually within the last twelve months, I do not suggest you share publicly. Wait until you have, at the very least, that amount of time of personal righteousness behind you.

- In the context of the church, your public announcement should only be done in conjunction with your local church leadership. Let these people help you craft your communiqué and assist you with your timing. I have found that those of us who come from a homosexual past often have an unintended edge to our words and the tone we use, based on a strong desire to teach and educate those who may have been insensitive with their words in the past. Your local minister has a plan for the direction of his church; work in unison with him, and trust the path and direction that he is laying out before you. If your local church leadership feels you should wait longer before making this public declaration, trust their guidance. To paraphrase Jerry McGuire, "help them help you!"

- Words matter. Be careful how you share your story. Be sensitive to younger people in the audience. Never share intimate details of your past. And it is not beneficial, in my estimation, for you as a Christian to ever describe yourself as being "gay" or "homosexual." I went into a very long explanation of this in a previous chapter entitled "Homosexuality Versus Same-Sex Attraction." Please read that chapter if you are considering going public with this news in your life.

Can a same-sex-attracted disciple serve in a children's program at church?

The issue here is not whether or not the person is a Christian, although I would assume any church would want to ensure that only Christians are teaching in their children's program; the issue is whether or not the individual is currently involved in homosexual activity. Any person who is acting out homosexually should not be involved in serving in any capacity around children.

Most homosexually attracted individuals suffer no unhealthy or sinful attractions toward children and would be repulsed at such a suggestion. As long as the Christian in question is clearly living a righteous life in this regard, they should be able to serve in this capacity.

As is always the case, anyone, no matter his or her background, should be carefully screened before being allowed to work around children.

I want to help and encourage same-sex-attracted Christians, but I fear that if I get too emotionally close, they might become attracted to me. Should I be concerned about this?

One of the beautiful aspects of Christianity is that we will have relationships that are close and honest and trusting, relationships in which we will indeed be bonded emotionally at a much deeper and meaningful level with the same gender than we would normally experience outside the Church. This is good and a part of God's plan for his people. In fact, for the same-sex-attracted disciple, there is almost nothing else that can assist in healing the emotional deficiencies left unmet in their youth than by being able to build healthy, nonsexual relationships with the same gender in a righteous environment.

My overall answer to this question is that you have nothing to fear. In my twenty-five year Christian experience as a same-sex-attracted individual, I have enjoyed the benefit of being emotionally connected with many, many Christian men, and I can confidently tell you that except for the rarest of occasions, there was never any physical attraction involved in my heart or mind, no matter how close the friendship became.

If you'll notice however, I did include "except for the rarest of occasions" in the above statement. That is to say, that in the last two and half decades, there have been those exceptional instances when I did know in my heart that if I were to continue developing this friendship, I could possibly form an unhealthy codependent relationship or physical attraction toward a certain Christian brother. When this has been the case, I have been exceedingly careful to put up appropriate boundaries such as decreasing the amount of time spent together, lessening the kind of influence that I allowed this person to have in my life, curtailing the kind of conversations we held, and most important, being completely transparent about this reality with a trusted spiritual advisor who committed to holding me accountable in this regard. Applying those boundaries, coupled with prayer, time and space, is all that is needed to set things right.

As a heterosexually attracted disciple, you should treat the Christian brother or sister who is attracted to the same gender in a similar manner as you would treat anyone else. These men and women are incredible individuals with gifts and talents and amazing qualities, not to mention the astonishing courage and bravery they have displayed by coming to Christ and changing for him. These are marvelous men and women, and your life will be blessed by getting to know them. You should have nothing to fear.

Does becoming a Christian affect the same-sex-attracted person's living arrangements? For instance, before becoming a disciple, if they lived with a same-sex partner, should that change if they have committed themselves to staying sexually pure after baptism? And what about other possible living conditions? Is it advisable that they live with other single men or women or with same-gender campus students?

Let me start this section by asking you to remember that it is never your responsibility as a Christian to force godly obedience, but rather to speak the truth in love and then walk alongside the individual as you continue to encourage them toward righteousness. With that being said, something that homosexual men and women must commit to, if they are going to become a Christian and truly experience real victory over impurity and homosexual activity, is to remove any and all avenues of homosexual behavior from their lives, including, in my estimation, any relationship that could cause them to stumble in their faith. This would most certainly include living arrangements where the person trying to become a Christian is living with a same-sex partner.

While I appreciate the heart that goes behind the commitment to be sexually pure if they were to continue living with their partner, this would be ignoring the fact that the physical side of the relationship is only one part of the bond that they would have built together. The other is the unhealthy emotional or relational connection they would have formed. It's important for Christians to not only abstain from inappropriate physical sexual contact, but also from any enmeshed emotional relationships that are not in line with biblical teaching. This would be almost impossible to accomplish while still living under the same roof as their ex-partner. It is therefore my belief that the living arrangements would indeed need to change.

With that being said, I realize that especially for relationships that have been together for an extended period of time, and particularly if children are involved, making such a decision would be incredibly difficult. As someone who is devoted to helping them, I would suggest you move very slowly and respectfully while you humbly yet honestly share your convictions and while you patiently wait for the Holy Spirit to work his will. It may take time for the person leaving homosexuality to take this step forward. Certainly you should douse the situation with prayer. Isaiah 30:18–21 tells us that it is God's heart and desire to help us when difficult decisions must be made. "Whether you turn to the right or to the left, your ears will hear a voice behind you, saying, 'This is the way; walk in it.'" Pray that God will move this person's heart so that they can have the faith, conviction and courage to do what is necessary.

As for whether or not a same-gender-attracted Christian should live with other same-gender single individuals, the short answer is "yes." However, I have had to counsel too many situations that became unhealthy to not offer my words of caution here. If a same-sex-attracted disciple is going to live with other single Christian people, appropriate boundaries must be in place. I would think that these boundaries are obvious, but surprisingly, they often are not.

- If at all possible, the same-sex-attracted disciple should have a bedroom to him- or herself. This may not always be possible, especially in a dormitory situation at school. That's all right; there's no reason why this living situation can't be done in a safe and righteous manner; if this is the case, then all the more reason why the next few pointers should be respected and followed.

- Roommates need to be considerate about the level of undress they allow themselves to be in outside of their own private living area in the home. No one should ever walk through the living quarters in the nude or even half-naked. That is not to suggest that the same-gender-attracted brother or sister would be attracted to that individual; they probably would not be, but out of respect, Christians should be wise in how they dress (or undress) in their home when living with a homosexually attracted disciple.

- A same-sex-attracted individual should never, and I mean not ever, share the same bed with someone of the same gender. I don't care how innocent people claim it is, trust me; I have counseled too many situations that started out apparently quite harmlessly but became something very harmful. I cannot imagine a situation where this would be a wise thing to do. I don't know how to be any clearer than that.

To my same-sex-attracted brothers and sisters: I realize it's difficult at times to have to live with so many boundaries and limitations. But let me remind you of the words of Peter in 1 Peter 1:13–20, a passage that I have turned to many, many times to remind me of the importance of my living righteously before God, regardless of how difficult it may seem to me at times.

Therefore, prepare your minds for action; be self-controlled; set your hope fully on the grace to be given you when Jesus Christ is revealed. As obedient children, do not conform to the evil desires you had when you lived in ignorance. But just as He who called you is holy, so be holy in all you do; for it is written: "Be holy, because I am holy."

Since you call on a Father who judges each man's work impartially, live your lives as strangers here in reverent fear. For you know that it was not with perishable things such as silver or gold that you were redeemed from the empty way of life handed down to you from your forefathers, but with the precious blood of Christ, a lamb without blemish or defect. He was chosen before the creation of the world, but was revealed in these last times for your sake.

My gay son or daughter wants to bring home his or her partner for the weekend. Should we allow this?

My first thought on this issue is that whatever you decide, it needs to be a family decision. Every adult living in the home needs to have had the opportunity to discuss their feelings on the issue and a consensus needs to be reached before a final decision is made on whether or not you allow your homosexual son or daughter to bring their same-sex partner home for an extended stay. My second thought is that as Christians, we are to be people of hospitality, and that hospitality should extend to people with whom we do not see eye to eye when it comes to God, the church and the Bible. I would think most parents would want their child to feel welcome at home at any time. Their home is always their home, even if they want to include their companion. You definitely should ask your child to respect the moral standards of your family. For most Christian homes, that would include boundaries such as no public displays of affection and that your child and their partner would sleep in separate bedrooms. I believe it would be safe to assume that if your child brought home an opposite-sex boyfriend or girlfriend for the weekend, you would most likely ask them to hold to these very same standards. Make sure your son or daughter knows this and that your requests are not based on their homosexuality, but on the morals of your home. If your child refuses to hold to those standards, then you should make it clear that they are welcome at any time, but not with their same-sex partner.

Probably the most difficult portion of allowing this to occur will be how you decide to treat your son's or daughter's companion. I would ask you to remember that this individual is not the enemy. The enemy is Satan, not your child or their same-sex partner. To truly have a positive impact on both your child and their friend, you must go out of your way to show kindness and love to this person. Do your best to make them feel welcome and a part of the family. Remember that this soul is just as lost as your child's and is in desperate need of God's grace and mercy in their lives. Pray that by spending time with your family, he or she will see Christ and maybe one day, after having built a loving and trusting relationship with you, ask you to teach them about the Lord. Such things are not too wild to consider. I have spoken with parents who have actually converted their child's partner to Christ. This can only occur through the parent showing unconditional love and acceptance to their child and to their child's same-sex partner.

I've been invited to a gay wedding or a "commitment ceremony" of some very good friends. I feel unsure how to respond. Would it be wrong to attend, considering what I believe the Bible to teach on this issue? Would accepting the invitation be misconstrued as approval of a relationship I think is sinful?

In today's cultural climate, traditional marriage is under attack from a very well-funded and forceful "gay rights" movement of activists who are intent on redefining the institution of marriage as something other than the joining of one man and one woman. The answer to this dilemma at first glance may seem obvious to you: a firm "No, thank you." And you may be right; we all have to live according to our conscience. But I would ask you to look at this topic through a set of different-colored lenses, the hue of which I think will permit you to accomplish this goal successfully without offending the inviter and in doing so be a worthy ambassador of Christ, holding to the biblical sexual ethic and staying true to your conscience.

So how would I suggest you proceed? Using the Great Commission as our guide, I suppose there are two primary questions that must be asked. The first question is this: What response to a gay wedding or commitment ceremony would most express Christian love and respect and allow the doors to be open for future dialogue and relationship? To answer this, I would suggest you consider this reality: Your rejection of the invitation will speak much louder than your acceptance. Chances are great that the individual inviting you will already know that you are a Christian. I can almost guarantee that this person would have already suffered a lifetime full of rejection and they most likely will have anticipated your negative response. With that in mind, I would suggest you accept the invite and go. The refusal to do so will only inhibit your ultimate objective, which is not to make a declaration in defense of the Bible by refusing, but to constantly find ways to build trust in this relationship so that you can eventually share the good news about Jesus and the Bible.

How can you do so in such a way that you are not giving in to tolerance and breaking your conscience? It's all in how *you* approach it in your own heart and mind, not in how the gay couple thinks of your attendance. I would encourage you to think of going to this ceremony in the context of being used by God to show love and to keep the doors of communication open as opposed to you supporting homosexuality. Your presence at the event does not have to mean that you are approving of gay marriage, but it can show that you are accepting of them as human beings, that you care about them as people and that you are willing to carry on a relationship with them in spite of their brokenness, even though they know you disagree with their choices in this regard. With this mindset, it is possible to attend such an event without adhering to society's definition of tolerance, whereby you tolerate everything and stand for nothing.

You can't affect people by only telling them what you are against. The whole idea of sharing the good news of Christ is to be able to bridge-build with a world that we know will do many things with which we do not agree. But how can we construct these bridges with people who need to hear this message if we aren't willing to be with them, live with them and mingle with them?

Christ did not approve of how the tax collectors, drunks and prostitutes lived, but that did not stop him from mixing with them, sharing meals with them and befriending them. There is a difference between acceptance and approval. We are all guilty of participating in multiple activities and thought patterns of which God most certainly does not approve, but he does unconditionally accept and love each one of us.

Attending a gay wedding or commitment ceremony does not mean that you have to approve of gay marriage or that you are giving way to gay activists intent on redefining the definition of marriage. In fact, the gay couple whose wedding you are attending are most likely not gay "activists," for that is but a tiny group in the gay community. Most likely the friends you are there to impact are just regular people, living their lives, not wanting to offend anyone. If the day ever comes that you are given the opportunity to share your biblical beliefs, you definitely should. The bottom line is always this: Jesus is better than anything homosexuality can provide; he's better than anything else, period. But how will you ever be able to share that reality if you have so offended everyone around you by your stance that they no longer care to hear what you have to say?

My viewpoint is that refusing to attend would only confirm people's prejudged idea of what a Christian would do, close down future dialogue and communication, and close the doors to you being able to effectively share the good news of Jesus with them in the future. I say go, having decided that your goal is to be a loving representative of Christ, as opposed to being one who fears that they are expressing tolerance of a union with which they disagree.

What stance should a Christian take on gay marriage?

I can't imagine many Christians actually arguing the point that marriage, as defined by God in Scripture, is not to be exclusively reserved to that between a man and a woman. The Bible is abundantly clear on this (Genesis 1:27, Genesis 2:22–24, Matthew 19:4–5, Ephesians 5:22–25, Mark 10:6–9).

When we're discussing same-sex marriage, it's critical that we clearly articulate what this debate is really about and what it's not about:

- It's not about whether gays and lesbians are nice people or good citizens. Some are, and some aren't, just like heterosexuals.

- It's not about whether gays and lesbians can conform to loving relationships—of course they can.

- It's not about whether gays and lesbians can be loving parents. There are nurturing, caring gay couples raising children all across the country.

- It's not about whether gays and lesbians should be treated with respect and dignity. Every member of the human race should be treated with respect and dignity.

Here's what I believe this debate is about:

- It's about whether we have the right to redefine marriage so it is elastic enough to include any groups of adults.

- It's about whether we acknowledge the wonderful human diversity expressed in the two sexes, male and female.

- It's about whether men and women compliment and complete each other in their differences.

- It's about whether mothers and fathers play unique and irreplaceable roles in the lives of children, precisely because of their sex.
- It's about whether there are compelling social reasons to define marriage as one thing and not as another.[3]

When it comes to the biblical worldview, a heterosexual, monogamous relationship as first presented in Genesis is the only model of sexual behavior consistently praised in both the Old and New Testaments. While it is true that other forms of sexual behavior like polygamy are allowed in the Old Testament, a committed relationship between husband and wife is the standard upheld as the ideal throughout all Scripture, and not once is homosexuality ever praised or left as an example of something that should be emulated.

Between the ages of nineteen and twenty-one, I lived in Papua New Guinea, a small island off the northern tip of Australia, which at the time was considered to be the most primitive place on earth. While there, I traveled to parts of the country that few Caucasians had ever been to before. It would not be an exaggeration to say that at that time (the early 1980s), there were tribes buried so deep in the jungles and mountains of that country that they still lived in Stone Age conditions, just as they had for thousands of years, almost completely untouched by modern society. I mention this when discussing the topic of gay marriage because I can tell you from firsthand experience that so universal and historically recognizable is this institution that even the pygmies of New Guinea, the vast majority of whom had no knowledge of the biblical worldview, knew instinctively that marriage was to be between a man and a woman (or as in the case of the Papua New Guinean pygmies, between a man and several women). No one had to teach them this standard; it was just as it had always been, for thousands of years. The Western-civilized world is undergoing what I believe is "the most radical social experiment ever proposed."[4] How this experiment will play out in years to come, and what consequences we will all suffer because of it, is yet to be fully realized.

With all of that being said, I suppose the real issue for the Christian is not whether or not gay marriage should be legal, but rather, how should the disciple of Christ deal with this social policy issue in the public square. In other words, to what degree should a Christian involve him- or herself in social reform?

We are given a unique insight into how the apostle Paul handled social reform in the culture in which he lived. In the book of Philemon, Paul writes to his friend Philemon about Onesimus, a slave from Colosse (Colossians 4:9) who had run away from his master, perhaps guilty of theft in the process (Philemon 18).

Onesimus was converted to Christ by Paul, and here Paul sends him back to his master with this letter, asking that he be welcomed back by his old master, not just as a slave but now as a dear brother in Christ.

In a very unique way, this letter actually deals with human slavery, yet as wrong and sinful as human slavery would have been to Paul and all of the Christians, the apostle does not attack slavery directly, for this is something the Christian communities of the first century were in no position to do; and the expectation that Christ would soon come again took away the urgency of being involved in social reform issues. Instead of attacking slavery, Paul spoke of love and mercy and forgiveness rather than involving himself in this social issue of his day. In other words, social reform was not the ideal and supreme purpose of his ministry; teaching people how to live righteously in the midst of a sinful society is what Paul tackled.

While I applaud those among us who do involve themselves in varying causes in our society in order to improve the lives of others, I think that overall, we as Christians would be wise not to allow social reform to be our ideal or top priority. While I'm sure it has its place at certain times, when it comes to issues like gay marriage, I'm not too confident that fighting against it in the public square is our place or that it should be our primary concern.

I do believe that compromise begets compromise, so I am not at all suggesting a loosening of the Biblical sexual ethic. As I have stated throughout this book, in the numerous articles I have authored in many different forums, and in the workshops I have taught publicly, Christians do need to boldly teach the standards that God has laid out for human sexuality; but I do also believe that this must be done with a huge sense of humility and kindness that will urge people to actually listen to what we have to say as opposed to using a combative tone that will only turn people away. For beyond all of the politics and arguments and public declarations and headlines are real people, with real lives and careers and friends and hurts and hobbies and bills and problems and parents and siblings, the majority of whom are not militant "activists," but rather everyday people who just want to live their lives peacefully. Most want to contribute to their communities; they want to make a positive difference in the world. They are kind and generous and wonderful human beings who also are in need of hearing the true message of Christ. I personally believe that if Christians make it their primary goal to tackle the issue of same-sex marriage in the public and political arenas, they will become more known for what they are against than what they are for. They will become identified as protestors more than Christians. They will end up speaking so loudly on social issues that the lost will not be willing to hear what they say when they do finally get around to speaking about Jesus.

Resources

1. Robert A. J. Gagnon, *The Bible and Homosexual Practice: Texts and Hermeneutics* (Nashville, TN: Abingdon Press, 2001).
2. Joe Dallas, *The Gay Gospel* (Eugene, OR: Harvest House, 2007).
3. Romell D. Weekly, *The Rebuttal: A Biblical Response Exposing the Deceptive Logic of Anti-Gay Theology* (Judah First Publishing, 2011).
4. Dan O. Via and Robert A. J. Gagnon, *Homosexuality and the Bible: Two Views* (Minneapolis, MN: Fortress Press, 2003).

Chapter Seven Endnotes

1. Jeff Buchanan, "What Does Exodus Believe About Genetics and Science?" December 18, 2009, http://www.exodusinternational.org/.

2. "Sexual Orientation and Homosexuality," The American Psychological Association, May 21, 2012, http://www.apa.org/helpcenter/sexual-orientation.aspx.

3. Bill Maier, "Same-Sex Marriage" in Joe Dallas and Nancy Heche, *The Complete Christian Guide to Understanding Homosexuality* (Eugene, OR: Harvest House, 2010), 364–65.

4. Ibid., 363.

Chapter Eight

Letters for Those Who Look for Strength in Weakness

To my dear same-sex-attracted brothers and sisters in Christ,

No one knows better than I do what you have struggled through as a same-sex-attracted follower of Jesus. I truly do stand in awe of the courage and strength that you have exhibited as you have stayed faithful to the Lord and to the promises you made to him when you became a Christian, regardless of how difficult it has been for you at times. I started my Strength in Weakness Ministry with you in mind. I had no idea what your name was and where in the world you resided, of course, but I knew that out there in our churches were men and women like me, disciples who loved God deeply and who were devoted to his church, but who also often felt like they were living beyond the margins, feeling isolated, misunderstood, confused, and with few places to turn to for practical assistance. If you have not yet seen our ministry, we are growing and changing all the time. I hope you will visit our website (www .strengthinweakness.org).

In our "Members Area" of our website, there are a series of Quiet Time Studies that I have authored specifically for same-sex-attracted Christians. Here I offer only six of the forty that are available there, but they are my six favorites. I do hope that you will find encouragement and reassurance in your Christian walk by reading them.

I pray for your every success!

—Guy Hammond
Executive Director
Strength in Weakness Ministries

Quiet Time #1

The Power to Become

There is a man you probably know very little about, yet without his accomplishments, our lives would be considerably different. His story is quite remarkable.

His name is George Washington Carver. In 1855 a white slave owner bought a thirteen-year-old girl named Mary. It is uncertain how many children Mary bore, but it is known that by her early twenties (due to the hard life conditions as a young slave girl in the southern United States) she had lost three children before they reached the age of ten. Her next child, George, was born during the U.S. civil war. His father was a slave on a neighboring farm who was killed in a logging accident shortly after George was born.

The western border of Missouri was the site of considerable guerilla warfare, and Mary and George along with the other slaves were prey to looting and killing by Confederate soldiers. Near the end of the war a group of men rode onto the land where they lived, in search of money. Mary and the infant George were kidnapped and taken into Confederate Arkansas. It was during this time that Mary, young, yet very old in her mid-twenties, died. So George Washington Carver grew up as a slave with no parents in the Deep South in the late 1800s.

Not a very auspicious beginning for anyone, is it? However, to make a long story short, George eventually won his freedom and as a young man got himself into school. He received a B.S. in 1894 and a M.S. in 1896 at the Iowa State College of Agriculture. He became a member of the faculty of Iowa State College of Agriculture and Mechanics in charge of the school's bacterial laboratory work in the Systematic Botany Department.

His work with agricultural resources developed industrial applications from farm products and soils. His research developed hundreds of products, many of which we use in our everyday lives even now. We owe to his genius the inventions of the following:

- Adhesives
- Bleach
- Chili sauce
- Dyes

- Hair shampoo
- Instant coffee
- Linoleum
- Meat tenderizer
- Metal polish
- Refined sugar
- Shaving cream
- Shoe polish
- Soil conditioner
- Synthetic rubber
- Talcum powder
- Vanishing cream
- Wood stains
- Wood filler

George Washington Carver was honored by U.S. President Franklin D. Roosevelt and a national park has been named after him. As well, he was bestowed an honorary doctorate from Simpson College and was made a member of the Royal Society of Arts in London, England.

Quite amazing, isn't it? All of this from a slave who was raised without parents in the abusive U.S. south of the late 1800s. George Washington Carver has gone down in history as one of the greatest minds of science the world has ever produced.

I love stories like this: of someone who beats the odds, who won't listen to the critics, who overcomes to become something that everyone else in the world would think impossible.

Paderewski, who is considered the greatest pianist of all time, was once advised by a celebrated teacher to give up all hope of ever becoming a concert pianist because: "There is just no talent there." Abraham Lincoln, before becoming President, had failed in business and gone bankrupt twice, lost eight elections, had a wife die, and even suffered a nervous breakdown. Beethoven was deaf. Yet all of these people believed that they had the power to become something different in spite of their difficulties.

One of the saddest sentences ever written comes from a poem by John Greenleaf Whittier: "For of all sad words of tongue or pen, the saddest are these: What might have been." The road of life is filled with many who end their lives wondering "what might have been," living their final years with regret. Isn't life too short for that? As a Christian that never need be the case.

We're going to spend just a few short minutes talking about who we have become as disciples and who we can become through the power of God. Yes, even for those of us who are same-gender attracted, so that we can get some vision about what God wants to do in our lives. Let's start with four small verses in John. In this passage we have a brief statement that shouts of triumph and victory:

> He was in the world, and though the world was made through him, the world did not recognize him. He came to that which was his own, but his own did not receive him. Yet to all who received him, to those who believed in his name, he gave the right to become children of God—children born not of natural descent, nor of human decision or a husband's will, but born of God.
>
> John 1:10–13

The NRSV translates verse 12 as: "But to all who received him, who believed in his name, he gave POWER TO BECOME children of God" (emphasis added).

God knows all too clearly what I am really like; he sees all the sin, the hurt, the insecurities, the warts and all. I don't know about you, but it is so easy for me when I look at who I really am before God, when my failures are glaring and naked for him to see, to feel like I am a failure and unable to do anything great with my life, especially in light of my same-gender attractions. Yet God, somehow, is able to see me, weaknesses and all, and believe that I can become so much more. In fact, he gives you and me the POWER to become so much more. While self-help books and books on psychology abound, and professional help from a therapist may have its role, absolutely nothing can take the place of God, who has in his very nature a desire to see us rise above, to conquer, to improve, and to become so much more than who and what we currently are. It is one thing for you to tell me that you believe I can become rich some day; it is something different for you to hand me a check to invest in my career or enterprise, and by that action you give me the power to become rich. So really, God is the one who "hands over the check."

The Bible is filled with this theme of God longing to do amazing things with our lives, regardless of how broken we have become. When Luke says in chapter 17 that the Kingdom of God is within us, what's that but another way of saying that we have the "power to become?" When Paul in Philippians 4:13 says that "[we] can do everything through him who gives [us] strength," what's that but another way of saying that we have the "power to become?" When John tells us that our faith overcomes the world (1 John 5:4), is he not telling us that we have the "power to become?"

When Jesus was in the world he always saw the potential in people. He saw people as diamonds in the rough, needing only to be refined and polished. This is how God looks at you! God sees that each of us possesses undreamed-of possibilities, pent-up skills and talents just crying out for discovery and release and development and exercise. As followers of Jesus, we need to look to our future with excitement and anticipation.

And don't think for a moment that potentiality is a respecter of age. Mozart composed a symphony when he was six, Shakespeare started writing when he was fourteen, Daniel was approximately just twelve years old when he was taken into cruel captivity by the Babylonians and Moses' work for God began when he was eighty. Young, middle-aged or old, God is not done with you yet!

And what of failure? History is full of great men and women who failed over and over again. Babe Ruth struck out 1,330 times but also got 714 home runs. John Creasey, the famous English novelist, got 753 rejection slips before he published any of his 534 books. Louis Pasteur made no fewer than 1,800 separate experiments, over a period of many hard years, before he ultimately succeeded in developing the technique of vaccination against anthrax. He began and failed, began and failed, began and failed eighteen hundred times, before he triumphed!

And so as Christians, we too are faced with our failures. If you're like me, you have repeated the same sins over and over again. Each time we have "repented," and before too long, sometimes the same day, we go right back to that sin. That's OK. God's forgiveness has no limit, and you cannot live as a Christian without learning how to successfully get up after you fall.

For though a righteous man falls seven times, he rises again, but the wicked are brought down by calamity.

Proverbs 24:16

This verse refers to the man or woman whose heart is committed to righteousness. We may sin, but it is our heart's desire to be righteous and obedient. If that is your heart, then the key is in getting up again. There is no glory or victory in staying down and quitting. When you fall and when you sin, run back to God, confess your sin, recommit yourself to following him again and get up and go.

Nothing in the world can take the place of persistence. Talent will not; nothing is more common than unsuccessful men with talent. Genius will not; unrewarded genius is almost a proverb. Education will not; the world is full of educated derelicts. Persistence and determination alone are omnipotent.

—Calvin Coolidge

There are few quotes more applicable to the Christian battle than just this one.

Every day we write another chapter of our lives. We have no power to rewrite yesterday's chapter, but each morning we have before us a blank sheet that will be filled one way or another. What are you writing today?

His divine power has given us everything we need for life and godliness through our knowledge of him who called us by his own glory and goodness. Through these he has given us his very great and precious promises, so that through them you may participate in the divine nature and escape the corruption in the world caused by evil desires.

2 Peter 1:3–4

"Participate in the divine nature." Isn't that incredible? Today, as you live your life, you get to actually participate in the divine nature of God! It doesn't matter who you used to be or who you are even today. Do you know why God asks, even expects that you deny yourself daily your temptations? Why? Because you can! He has given you everything you need for holiness. He has given you everything you need to escape the corruption and evil desires of same-gender attraction.

God expects you today:

To be holy—BECAUSE YOU CAN!
To be pure—BECAUSE YOU CAN!
To conquer your feelings, moods and emotions—BECAUSE YOU CAN!
To be self-controlled—BECAUSE YOU CAN!

As Christians who live with unwanted same-gender attractions, you need to know that with God, you need not remain stagnant. Whether or not your sexual orientation ever changes is not the point, nor do I personally think this should be considered the pinnacle of your success as a Christian.

It's not like heterosexuals have cornered the market on righteousness, that they have no issues to work through, or that they have reached a level of godliness unattainable to you and me. Is God's grace not sufficient? If it was sufficient for the thorn in Paul's life, whatever that was, is that same grace not sufficient for same-gender attracted disciples as well? Don't focus on what you're attracted too, for it doesn't matter, and God is not concerned about it. What he is concerned about is your holiness, your righteousness. The goal of your life should not be to become heterosexual; it should be to become holy.

Should the day ever come that the Lord decides to zap this particular problem out of your life, congratulations, but if you receive that blessing will you still not have many, many more temptations and character flaws to deal with? Having your same-gender attractions vanish will hardly make you perfect and temptation free, so stop worrying about it. Switching from one kind of temptation (homosexual lust) to another kind of temptation (heterosexual lust) is not the goal here. The key will not be your sexual orientation, but rather your righteousness and the determination to stay faithful to the end—which you never quit.

God has a plan for your life, things he wants to accomplish through you. You can and will grow, change and mature from where you are right now, because of you being with God. He has given us the power to become more than what we are today, and that has nothing to do with what you're attracted to.

May we all live our lives in such a way that when our life enters its "winter season," when the end draws nigh, no one, including ourselves, will ever be able to look at what we accomplished and say those awful words, "Oh, what might have been," but rather, "Wow, look at what that person became by the power of God!"

> Not that I have already obtained all this, or have already been made perfect, but I press on to take hold of that for which Christ Jesus took hold of me. Brothers, I do not consider myself yet to have taken hold of it. But one thing I do: Forgetting what is behind and straining toward what is ahead, I press on toward the goal to win the prize for which God has called me heavenward in Christ Jesus.
>
> Philippians 3:12–14

Quiet Time #2

The Valley of Baca

We're going to talk about a place mentioned only twice in all of Scripture. If you've read through the Psalms or Judges, you would have read about this location, but it's a place that has escaped my attention and I have rarely thought about it.

This place is a valley just outside of Jerusalem. I want to talk about this little valley because what occurred there can provide us with some valuable insight into our Christian walk. The valley is called "the Valley of Baca."

As I said, the valley of Baca is named only twice in the Bible. The first mention is our main text:

> Blessed are those whose strength is in you,
>   who have set their hearts on pilgrimage.
> As they pass through the Valley of Baca,
>   they make it a place of springs;
>   the autumn rains also cover it with pools.
>
> Psalm 84:5–6

"Baca" is a Hebrew word that means "weeping." Therefore, the valley of Baca means literally the "valley of weeping." Where did this valley get its name? It's an odd name for a valley.

> The angel of the LORD went up from Gilgal to Bokim and said, "I brought you up out of Egypt and led you into the land that I swore to give to your forefathers. I said, 'I will never break my covenant with you, and you shall not make a covenant with the people of this land, but you shall break down their altars.' Yet you have disobeyed me. Why have you done this? Now therefore I tell you that I will not drive them out before you; they will be thorns in your sides and their gods will be a snare to you."
>
> When the angel of the LORD had spoken these things to all the Israelites, the people wept aloud, and they called that place Bokim [or Baca]. There they offered sacrifices to the LORD.
>
> Judges 2:1–5

The Israelites were in the midst of driving their enemies out of the land of Canaan. But they intermarried with the enemy (and at times worshipped their gods), so after the death of Joshua, the Lord sent an angel to rebuke the Israelites for their insubordination and wickedness.

At the time of the rebuke they were encamped in a valley. So severe was the rebuke, so hurtful the punishment that the people (literally millions of them) broke down and wept. The crying and wailing was so intense that the valley was given the name "the Valley of Baca" or, "the Valley of Weeping."

Now when you read the account in Judges, it says that the angel just "said" some things to them. It hardly seems like a rebuke when you read the account. However, I'm quite confident that when an angel of God rebukes you, it must be an absolutely terrifying event that would be cataclysmic enough to make any of us weep and wail.

Now today, geographically, there is actually a valley that exists with the same name in southern Lebanon. In fact, it is exactly in the area that is still a hotly contested area, and in 2007 the Hezbollah dug itself in and fought Israel over it. That area is called the Baca Valley. However, the world's most authentic geographers and historians seem generally agreed that the Valley of Weeping that we read about in Psalms and Judges was geographically situated near Jerusalem, not in Southern Lebanon.

Now in Psalm 84:5–6, the writer is saying that the person who is set on a pilgrimage through this valley should be blessed. So, going through the valley of tears is actually a good thing!

Blessed are those whose strength is in you,
who have set their hearts on pilgrimage.
As they pass through the Valley of Baca,
they make it a place of springs;
the autumn rains also cover it with pools.

When you picture a valley, you think of it as being a picturesque place between beautiful mountains with colorful flowers blanketing the hillsides. Kind of like that scene in the movie *The Sound of Music* with Julie Andrews swirling around singing "The Hills Are Alive."

Take that picture out of your mind. The Valley of Baca has no resemblance to that image, whatsoever. Throughout the centuries, this area outside of Jerusalem was and still is a dry, barren desert, a terrible stretch of land through which one had to travel on his journey to Jerusalem to get to the temple to worship. Indeed, the prospect was not a very pleasant one, for to journey through Baca meant fatigue and hardship and hunger and thirst.

So why, then, does the psalmist say that those who are on a pilgrimage and who must go through the valley of tears are actually blessed? How can traveling through a hot, dry and barren land that causes pain, hunger, thirst and tears be a good thing?

For the man or woman who wanted to get to Jerusalem to worship God, the joy and determination to carry on through this terrible place, the valley of weeping, was that once you got to the other side, Jerusalem was waiting. The temple where God lived was waiting for your arrival. Speaking metaphorically, the Valley of Baca is actually none other than life's valley of weeping that we all must go through to successfully reach the other side, where God waits.

In society, in our own personal lives and sometimes even in the church, we are led to believe that pain is a bad thing that should be avoided at all costs. In my Christian walk I have tried to cover over the pain I may feel by making myself busier, praying more, doing more Bible study or telling myself I just need more faith. I can turn to entertainment, sleep, fun, joking or self-indulgence of some kind that often results in only further sin—whatever I have to do to avoid going beneath the surface to really deal with the things that God wants me to deal with.

The idea of talking about the necessity of going through our valley of weeping to get to God came from a phone call I received last week from an old friend in Toronto. The man is not a Christian and has rarely shown any interest in becoming one, in spite of my best attempts over these last twenty years. Currently, he is going through a difficult time financially, and he called me to see if I would do a "prosperity prayer" with him over the phone.

He had seen on Vision TV some televangelists preaching the common and popular false doctrine that Christianity is for wealth and health, that following Jesus is more for what we can get out of life now instead of a journey to know God, whatever the cost, so that we can enjoy what we will receive after this life. It is a teaching that says that God is here to relieve us of the pain of living in a fallen world.

But I disagree with that doctrine. I believe that it is not only acceptable to hurt and struggle in our hearts, but even necessary. We're not Christians for health and wealth. We're Christians because we want to know God.

The Valley of Weeping for the Israelites in Judges 2 was a place of rebuke, conviction and repentance. It was necessary for them to weep. The Valley of Weeping for the early Jewish pilgrim was a place that they had to travel through in order to get to the city of God and find his temple. It was a necessary trip for them to make to see God.

The valley of weeping for you and me is a place that we must go through in order that we might get closer to God. The valley of weeping is a lesson: You and I cannot be afraid of facing our sadness, our hidden sin or the pain that comes from brokenness. With God, fewer statements are truer than "no pain, no gain." In fact, this whole physical world and the physical bodies in which we live are not our real home for the Christian. Our real home is heaven with God.

It's like living in a motel. There is a bed to sleep on, a TV to watch and a few modern comforts, but it's just a motel. It's not home. So even though we must stay at the motel when we are traveling, it's not a place we want to stay at. It's just a stopover place that we have to stay at on our journey.

That's what being a Christian is like.

Like the motel, this world is a place we must stop at and stay for a while until we check out and go home. It offers some nice conveniences at times, but for the most part, we're not really happy here; we don't really want to be here. It's expensive, it's uncomfortable, the people are often not very nice and the remote rarely works. It would be strange if you loved staying in motels and didn't want to go home. Likewise, it would be strange if we loved this motel called life, when home is really with God.

Therefore, this life is just a place we are passing through. It's not supposed to be a place that we love so much we can't imagine leaving. In today's modern Christian circles, the idea that Christianity is a life of worry-free living filled with prayers of prosperity for physical wealth and a pain-free life is a false and shallow religion.

For the Christian, beneath the surface of our lives, there should be an ache that will not go away. It can be ignored, disguised, mislabeled or submerged by a torrent of activity, but it will not disappear. And for good reason: We were designed to enjoy a better world than this. And until that better world comes along, we will groan for what we do not have.

An aching soul is evidence of our understanding that we are spiritual beings in a physical and sinful world that is not our home. Today the "valley of weeping" has become a figure of speech rather than a place on the map, and I know that I have been there many times. But I look back now over the past twenty-five years and can clearly see that when I was going through my times of weeping, I grew the most spiritually.

I have been in the valley of bereavement from the death of my father. All of us have gone through this valley in one way or another. For the Christian, just when you think you can't take the pain any longer, Jesus calls out and says, "Do not let your hearts be troubled....In my Father's house are many rooms."

There is the valley of disillusionment. But when my dreams have been broken and my heart along with them, when I no longer believed in myself and have felt like a failure, God has always called back and said, "For I know the plans I have for you,...plans to prosper you and not to harm you, plans to give you hope and a future."

There is the valley of repentance. This is a valley I know all too well. Repentance is always difficult. It requires you to have an honest and humble look at yourself. It requires a broken and contrite heart before God. It requires confession, openness, transparency and shame. True repentance requires pain and weeping. Anyone who says they have dealt with their sin but has shed no tears, physically or emotionally, in the effort has not dealt with their sin and truly repented.

I cannot relate to a man who has not been in the valley. I see people who seem to sail through their Christianity with little struggle and little temptation and I can only envy them, I think. Or maybe not! Come to think of it, people like that disturb me. They look so together. I don't know if they are really that successful or are in denial.

My valleys have included the crushing weight of bad news and the overwhelming feeling of being spiritually drained with no desire to carry on. In my valley I have wrestled with my own inability to handle tough decisions; I have fought nagging doubts and lived with fears, insecurities and worries about the future; I have carried a heaviness of heart about those in my church who are struggling; and I have a constant sense of being overwhelmed by the number of lost around me and the enormity of the job to evangelize the geographic area that I live in. And then there is my own sinful nature that I can never seem to truly kill once and for all: the temptations to lust, the desire to sin, the sometimes overwhelming deep feeling that I need homosexual contact to make me feel loved and accepted—the lies that Satan whispers.

A while back a brother asked me to meet him at six a.m. to go on a prayer walk. While I was not expecting it to occur, he forced me into the valley. I spent some time complaining about some problems I was facing, and in this I was confronted with my sinful attitudes that I had been harboring toward some other people. While in the valley, my heart was so convicted that I spent four hours in prayer and Bible study. It was not fun in the valley, being rebuked and having my heart convicted and challenged, but I needed to go there so that I could repent.

Valleys of weeping are actually good things to go through as a Christian because they actually force us to our knees. They force us to depend not on ourselves but on God. They force us to see that we can't do this alone.

And let us remember: We do not need to walk in the valley alone. We are our "brothers' keepers." As Paul said, we must "carry each other's burdens" (Gal 6:2). Let me remind you of what we have already studied. As it says in Ecclesiastes 4:10, "If one falls down, his friend can help him up. But pity the man who falls and has no one to help him up!"

These valleys of tears force us to turn not only to our brother or sister for help, but also to God.

> To this you were called, because Christ suffered for you, leaving you an example, that you should follow in his steps.
>
> 1 Peter 2:21

> Consider it pure joy, my brothers, whenever you face trials of many kinds, because you know that the testing of your faith develops perseverance. Perseverance must finish its work so that you may be mature and complete, not lacking anything.
>
> James 1:2

James here gives us a spiritual equation, a formula for the growth of souls. Show me a man or woman who has not struggled in the valley, and I'll show you a shallow Pharisee who is smug, self-righteous, fake and unrelatable.

Show me a man or woman who while in the valley of weeping has been forced to their knees in prayer and forced to be humble with both God and man, and I'll show you a person who has produced those beautiful intangible qualities: humility, unselfishness, sympathetic understanding, patience, a nonjudgmental heart, compassion for those hurt and forgiveness. Thousands upon thousands of spiritually immature Christians enter the valley, but few ever leave it in the same condition.

Let us remember that Jesus lived in this valley. It was because of his tears that he could show so much compassion to those hurting. When he was in the Garden of Gethsemane begging God to rescue him, he was in the valley of tears. When Jesus suffered the whipping and beating before the crucifixion, he was in the valley of weeping. When the Lord hung on the cross as people mocked him, he thought of you and me and our sin and went through the valley of weeping.

Finally, I think we ought to be encouraged by a preposition that the Psalmist uses both here in Psalm 84 and in Psalm 23. Psalm 23 says, "Though I walk through the valley of the shadow of death, I will fear no evil." "Through" is the key word. In fact, it is the key word of the Christian life. If that seven-letter preposition were omitted from the text, life would be meaningless and futile. We don't walk "into" the valley, but we walk "through" the valley of shadows and tears. We walk into it, we travel through it, but with God, we always walk out of it.

And God shall wipe away all tears from their eyes.

Rev. 21:4a KJ21

Quiet Time #3

How to Deal With Guilt

According to this ad, it is possible to live guilt free!

Don't worry be happy sounds like a dream? No, really, worry and guilt are two man made emotions. ....These man made emotions cheat us out of the here and now....This one cd program takes the worry, anxiety and guilt trips...and dissolves them...a full proof [sic] means to become your own best friend....Overcoming guilt is easy as you learn to live in the here and now with the revolutionary cognitive skills that gives you the key to becoming your own best friend....Overcoming guilt is like a walk in the park on a beautiful spring day....Get Rid of Worry and Guilt CD $24.95. On sale now for only $14.95. Money Back Guarantee!

Well, I suppose this is one way of dealing with your guilt. But let me save you $14.95 and offer you some suggestions from the Bible on how to deal with your guilt.

Canadians have an addiction to three things: hockey, beer and coffee. In fact, one of Canada's most recognized and iconic companies is a coffee shop started by and named after a famous hockey player. Millions of Canadians can't start their day without a cup of coffee from Tim Hortons. A while back I was out making my daily pilgrimage when I asked the girl behind the counter if she would like to come to church. I told her the topic was going to be on how to deal with guilt. In response she said, "Oh, I know all about guilt; my life is filled with it." I appreciate her honesty. The fact is, this emotion is something we all feel in our gut.

Encarta defines the word as: "an awareness of having done wrong or committed a crime, accompanied by feelings of shame and regret."

A life filled with guilt is no way to live. Guilt can drain us spiritually, emotionally and physically. Ultimately, this hinders us from living as the men and women God designed us to be. If this kind of guilt characterizes your life, I hope this lesson and the next one, on shame, will provide a lasting hope.

The story is told of the famous English actor and playwright named Noel Coward, who wanted to play a prank on some people he wasn't quite fond of. He wrote an anonymous letter that was identical in its content to ten notable and highly decorated men in London, England. Here is what he said: "We know what you have done. If you don't want to be exposed, leave town." Within six months, all ten men who had received the letter had actually moved!

How would we respond to receiving an anonymous letter saying, "We know all about what you have done; leave town"? I wonder how many of us would be scrambling to get the number to U-HAUL.

There are two different kinds of guilt, and I want to make it clear, first of all, what we are specifically talking about here. There is a "social guilt": a guilt that is placed upon us that has nothing to do with our actions, but rather with our own or others' expectations.

For instance, some cultures put a huge value on education and career choice, which in turn places an enormous amount of guilt on the young person who wants to go to acting school but whose parents want them to go to law school. This simply means that if you choose acting anyway, you will remain guilty for life. Some people just feel guilty for saying "No." In doing so, even though they did nothing wrong, they now feel guilty—therefore a social construct in their mind has caused this guilt to unnecessarily burden them. This is not the kind of guilt we are talking about here.

But there is another kind of guilt that comes when we violate our conscience, when we do something we know we should not have done, and now our heart feels the pang of guilt. To cover this intense pain, many find themselves on a quest to avoid being put in situations where they will be judged or examined in any way.

Most of us turn up the volume on life, thinking that perhaps if we absorb more into our minds and schedules, then possibly the loudness of life might dull the pain of guilt we feel. So we cram more into our already overwhelmed schedules, so that there is no time to stop and think and feel. The parent who is guilty about not spending enough time with the kids will run out and buy them more "stuff" to dull the pain.

When it comes to our struggles with homosexuality, there is plenty of guilt to go around! But as a Christian, what role should guilt play in our lives? There is a biblical method of removing that awful feeling from our hearts. I want to offer two steps to removing guilt from our lives.

Easy Step #1: Draw Closer to God

Hebrews 10:22 tells us to "draw near to God with a sincere heart in full assurance of faith, having our hearts sprinkled to cleanse us from a guilty conscience." The Greek word translated "conscience" means "to be one's own witness." It is "self-awareness." It is saying the conscience is like an inside man casting a vote about the rightness or wrongness of our behaviors.

Paul spoke of possessing a clear conscience numerous times, yet he considered himself one of the worst possible offenders. His conscience was clear even though he had wronged many people in the past; this is good news! If your sins are not forgiven, then it is understandable that you feel guilty. Consider yourself fortunate that you feel guilt.

> "Now I am going to him who sent me, yet none of you asks me, 'Where are you going?' Because I have said these things, you are filled with grief. But I tell you the truth: It is for your good that I am going away. Unless I go away, the Counselor will not come to you; but if I go, I will send him to you. When he comes, he will convict the world of guilt in regard to sin and righteousness and judgment: in regard to sin, because men do not believe in me; in regard to righteousness, because I am going to the Father, where you can see me no longer; and in regard to judgment, because the prince of this world now stands condemned."
>
> John 16:5–11

God loves us too much not to try and get our attention. This guilt we feel comes from God and is for our benefit. When someone has a lack of guilt, they have no motivation to abide by God's commands. God created in the architecture of our hearts a conscience, a soil in which he can plant and imbed truths. It is more than emotion; it is more than intellect; our conscience causes us to feel remorse for wrong behavior.

The Holy Spirit plays a critical role in working with our conscience, and we must invite the Holy Spirit to work. Romans 1 tells us of a group of people who sinned so many times that there was no more guilt; they had exchanged the truth for a lie! We should be really grateful to have the Holy Spirit make his presence known and be prompting and warning and nudging and tugging on our hearts.

Guilt is a sign that there is still hope, that there is still a spark that can lead to a flame. This sort of guilt does not enslave; it creates a sorrow that brings us to the feet of Jesus. But when we come to the feet of Jesus, what will he do with us? There is no greater story to me personally that shows how Jesus longs to deal with us in our guilt than this one:

> But Jesus went to the Mount of Olives. At dawn he appeared again in the temple courts, where all the people gathered around him, and he sat down to teach them. The teachers of the law and the Pharisees brought in a woman caught in adultery. They made her stand before the group and said to Jesus, "Teacher, this woman was caught in the act of adultery. In the Law Moses commanded us to stone such women. Now what do you say?" They were using this question as a trap, in order to have a basis for accusing him.
>
> But Jesus bent down and started to write on the ground with his finger. When they kept on questioning him, he straightened up and said to them, "If any one of you is without sin, let him be the first to throw a stone at her." Again he stooped down and wrote on the ground.
>
> At this, those who heard began to go away one at a time, the older ones first, until only Jesus was left, with the woman still standing there. Jesus straightened up and asked her, "Woman, where are they? Has no one condemned you?"
>
> "No one, sir," she said.
>
> "Then neither do I condemn you," Jesus declared. "Go now and leave your life of sin."
>
> John 8:1–11

The scribes and Pharisees were out to get some charge on which they could discredit Jesus, and here they thought they caught him in quite a dilemma. In the eyes of Jewish law, adultery was a serious crime. Adultery was, in fact, one of the three gravest sins and punishable by death. From the purely legal point of view, the scribes and Pharisees were perfectly correct. This woman was liable to death by stoning.

The dilemma into which they sought to put Jesus was this: If he said that the woman ought to be stoned to death, he would lose the name he had gained for love and mercy and never again would be called the friend of sinners. The scribes and Pharisees insisted on an answer—and they got it. Jesus said in effect: "All right! Stone her! But let the man who is without sin be the first to cast a stone."[1]

The words for "without sin" mean not only without sin, but even without a sinful desire. Jesus was saying: "Yes, you may stone her—but only if you never wanted to do the same thing yourselves." There was a silence—and then slowly the accusers drifted away.[2]

So Jesus and the woman were left alone. Can you imagine the enormous guilt that this poor woman must have been going through as she stood there alone, having been caught in the middle of a sexual embrace with a man who wasn't her husband, no doubt naked, except for maybe a sheet that was quickly grabbed off the bed to try to hide herself in? She was guilty. To the legal experts of the day it was clear that authority was characteristically critical, that guilt should be capitalized on, and that punishment should be the only option. It never entered their heads that authority should be based on mercy or that its aim should be to help save people when they are in trouble and to relieve them of their guilt.

Yet we find here in Jesus the "gospel of the second chance." He was always intensely interested, not only in what a person had been, but also in what a person could be. The basic difference between Jesus and the scribes was that they wished to condemn and take advantage of guilt; he wished to forgive and relieve people of guilt. They knew the thrill of exercising the power to condemn; Jesus knew the thrill of exercising the power to forgive and heal.

When he was confronted with someone who had gone wrong, he did not say, "You are a wretched and hopeless person." He said essentially, "I know you can do better, so go, and sin no more." His method was not to blast people with the knowledge—which they already possessed—that they were miserable sinners, but to inspire them with the unbelievable discovery that they were potential saints.

Easy Step # 2: Examine the Source of the Guilt

> Then he showed me Joshua the high priest standing before the angel of the Lord, and Satan standing at his right side to accuse him. The Lord said to Satan, "The Lord rebuke you, Satan! The Lord, who has chosen Jerusalem, rebuke you! Is not this man a burning stick snatched from the fire?"
>
> Now Joshua was dressed in filthy clothes as he stood before the angel. The angel said to those who were standing before him, "Take off his filthy clothes."
>
> Then he said to Joshua, "See, I have taken away your sin, and I will put rich garments on you."
>
> Then I said, "Put a clean turban on his head." So they put a clean turban on his head and clothed him, while the angel of the Lord stood by.
>
> Zechariah 3:1–5

The name "Satan" literally means accuser. Satan the accuser wants to imprison us, to destroy our confidence. He will accuse us of things both real and imagined. Satan's biggest reason for accusing us is the hope that we will stop short of our potential; he wants to limit our growth and maturity in Christ. For the Christian, and this has certainly been the case in my life, Satan's accusations are often persistent. They throb like a spiritual migraine at times. They have tormented me even after I have acknowledged known wrongs and asked God for forgiveness. Can you relate?

I have found it a most helpful practice at those times to think through my feelings of guilt and to logically consider why I am feeling guilty and where these feelings are coming from, either from God or Satan. You really only have two choices.

Whenever you are overwhelmed by feelings of guilt, stop and ask: Why am I feeling guilty? Is there a sin I have committed that the Holy Spirit is convicting me of and that I have yet to truly repent of? Am I cherishing sin in my heart? Is there sin I have yet to confess to God or to man? (James 5:16). If after honestly considering these questions you discover that there is no hidden sin and you have been truthful and transparent with others, then your feelings of guilt are not from God.

Whenever we are overwhelmed by guilt feelings that aren't traceable to a specific sin, or whenever feelings of condemnation persist even after we have honestly confessed sin to the Lord and repented, it is reasonable to assume that we are suffering from false guilt—guilt that is coming from our spiritual enemy.

The Bible tells us that godly conviction is based on love, not fear. God's purpose is to instruct and to correct, not to torment. The apostle John wrote in 1 John 4:18, "There is no fear in love. But perfect love drives out fear, because fear has to do with punishment." God is not arbitrary or cruel. He always convicts his children out of love, not anger and frustration. Conviction is his tool to bring us to a deeper reliance upon Christ. His Spirit doesn't overwhelm us with feelings of condemnation for sins that have been confessed and repented of.

In this fallen world, we will always struggle with some legitimate feelings of guilt. Here we wrestle with the tension of knowing that everything we do falls short of perfection. But our faith must trust God's promises. We must be willing to go forward in spite of uncertainty and to be as fearless of God's wrath as a child is of a loving Father.

Satan, on the other hand, wants to twist you into a knot of torment; he has duped society into evaluating our level of success by reaching certain achievement markers. He wants us to feel guilty and stay paralyzed in this present age whose rules run contrary to the will of God.

Are you feeling guilty? Are you being held in chains by past failures? Then is the Holy Spirit convicting you of sin? Now is the time to come to God and confess your sins as one who needs God.

Have you been forgiven by God already but still the thoughts and memories of yesterday's sins confuse your life? If after confessing our sin and acknowledging the truth of God's word that we are forgiven, we still feel guilt, then that is an indicator that we have turned our focus away from God's forgiveness and mercy and onto ourselves. We are saying that our sinful weakness is more powerful than God's forgiving power. Either he isn't big enough to forgive us or he doesn't want to forgive us, both of which are untrue.

God wants you to bring your guilt and heavy conscience to him. Spill your heart and confess everything you feel. Tell him about the guilt that continues to nag at you. You'll not only clear your heart and mind; you'll bind up the strong man who has no right to keep accusing you after repentance.

In his word, God tells you over and over how much he loves you. He assures you of forgiveness. He also tells you that he forgets your confessed sin. Ask God to give you faith to take him at his word so that you need not fear rejection or ridicule. Let him reassure you of his love and forgiveness. Was Christ's death on the cross enough to cover your sin, enough to take away your guilt? Yes. He gave everything he had for everything we've said, done or thought. Let us draw near to God and let us stop listening to the accuser.

Quiet Time #4

How to Deal With Shame

We know that the law is spiritual; but I am unspiritual, sold as a slave to sin. I do not understand what I do. For what I want to do I do not do, but what I hate I do. And if I do what I do not want to do, I agree that the law is good. As it is, it is no longer I myself who do it, but it is sin living in me. I know that nothing good lives in me, that is, in my sinful nature. For I have the desire to do what is good, but I cannot carry it out. For what I do is not the good I want to do; no, the evil I do not want to do—this I keep on doing. Now if I do what I do not want to do, it is no longer I who do it, but it is sin living in me that does it.

So I find this law at work: When I want to do good, evil is right there with me. For in my inner being I delight in God's law; but I see another law at work in the members of my body, waging war against the law of my mind and making me a prisoner of the law of sin at work within my members. What a wretched man I am! Who will rescue me from this body of death? Thanks be to God—through Jesus Christ our Lord!

Romans 7:14–25a

With this passage we find some of the most brutally honest and heart-felt words penned by any man, and I must say one of the most moving passages in Scripture, because here Paul is giving us his own spiritual autobiography and laying bare his very heart and soul.

Here Paul deals with the torturing paradox of God's law. In themselves, God's laws are holy; they come from a sphere other than this world. God's laws are divine and have in them the very voice of God. And so we see here a man who is baring his very soul, and he is telling us of an experience that we all can relate to, one that speaks of the very essence of the human condition. Paul knew what was right, he wanted to do what was right, and yet, somehow, he kept doing what was wrong. Paul knew what was wrong and the last thing he wanted to do was to do it, and yet, somehow, he did it.

Whenever I read that scripture I can so relate to the pain that Paul felt. I have dedicated the last twenty-three years of my life to trying to be a godly man, to obeying the scriptures, to living how God has asked me to live, but in spite of my best efforts, I fail, and sometimes miserably. The whole process shows us the ugliness of sin. Sin can take the beauty of love and turn it into lust. Sin can take the honorable desire for independence and turn it into the ache for money and power. Sin can lead us down horrible roads where we end up saying and doing things we at one time would have said were impossible. There are few areas where this is more true than in homosexuality.

It leads us to cross lines that we never thought we'd cross. We end up saying or thinking or doing things so awful that we wish so badly we could take back but never can. Things that we keep hidden and locked in our hearts because what we did was so bad that if anyone found out, if our friends or siblings, if our husbands or wives, if our children or parents, if anyone in the church or if our coworkers knew, we would be mortified. And so the doors to our hearts get shut and locked, the key is thrown away, and only we know. Deep down inside who we really are in our hearts, we live with something called "shame."

To say the least, I am not proud of the homosexual acts that I participated in; they were shameful and disgusting. If I could magically go back and erase those moments from my life, I gladly would, but I can't. The toothpaste is out of the tube, and there's no way of ever changing that. Over the years I have bemoaned and mourned those foolish and embarrassing events. For years I kept them locked deep in my heart, where they rotted and caused me grief. It took a long time, but I finally realized that there is only one appropriate place for my shame: left at the feet of Jesus.

In the previous study we read in John 8:1–11 about the woman caught in the act of adultery. Please go back and read that again, if you need a refresher. I don't think there was anyone more damaged by shame than this poor, guilty woman. Like all of us, she got bamboozled by Satan into believing his lies, the same lies we all tell ourselves when we are tempted to sin.

Tell me if you haven't thought these thoughts: "No one will know," "My sin isn't really hurting anyone," "This will make me feel better," "I know it's wrong, but God will forgive me," "This will heal the ache of my heart."

I find it interesting that religious leaders dragged her (not the man) to what she surely would have believed to be the end of her life. As they yanked her through the streets, she no doubt started to attract a crowd. That's what other people's sin does; it gets everyone's attention; it gets everyone talking; it's like an accident on the side of the highway that people slow down to see. Everyone wants to see the mess.

She must have been thinking, "I know what's next; the law is clear: They are going to take me to the edge of the cliff, throw me down and then hurl stones on me until I'm dead." But I put before you that at this point it wasn't death she feared the most, it was the humiliation and the shame: "What will my friends say; what will my husband say; this is not how I want my parents and my children to remember me."

But in the midst of this horrible scene, as if the situation could not have worsened for this poor soul, it did: Instead of taking her to the cliff, they made a turn away from the hill and started toward the temple. With absolute horror, the woman realized that they were taking her to the house of God! She must have gasped, "Please, not there, not to the temple, not to the church! I'm guilty; I deserve death; do whatever you want to me, but please, don't expose me there!"

But then the situation turned even more dire, for when they arrived at the temple they came to a crowd of people who had already gathered. Here they pushed this half-naked woman through that crowd, and suddenly she found herself standing in front of Jesus, the living

Son of God. She was guilty, but now she had to stand before the sinless, Holy God. This was more than an embarrassment; this was shame in the deepest sense.

In our study on guilt, we saw how it is something that God uses to motivate us to change. In fact, guilt (in this sense) is a good thing, because it means that you are alive, that there is a fire in there, and that there is hope. Shame, likewise, has its merit, as it can be a reminder to you of what you were intended to be. Certainly shame can be a double-edged sword, but there is a healthy aspect that says: "You were made for something better."

Shame is different from guilt. At least guilt is tied to sin, and it is therefore something you can confess and repent of, but shame is deeper than that. Shame says, "It is not just that I did something wrong, but there is something wrong with me for participating in this sin."

I learned that shame doesn't change because you repent. Shame can linger and the only way it can truly be dealt with is that it must be left at the feet of Jesus. Jesus knew all about shame. Hebrews 12:2 says: "Let us fix our eyes on Jesus, the author and perfecter of our faith, who for the joy set before him endured the cross, scorning its shame, and sat down at the right hand of the throne of God."

Today, at least in Western society, the cross is a perfectly acceptable symbol, a rather harmless token of the Christian faith. But originally, the cross was one of the most degraded and debased symbols imaginable. In the earliest days of the church, the cross was not only perceived by society as both an instrument of torture and death, but also as a symbol of utter shame. In the ancient mind, crucifixion (and the cross as its symbol), was regarded as both vile and vulgar. When you wanted to really insult and hurt someone, the term crucifixion was used quite literally as a curse word. Crucifixion was clearly understood to be the crudest and most dishonorable form of death. So the concept of a perfect God dying such a death was absolutely ludicrous.

Perhaps we don't understand that ancient mentality of hostility toward the preaching of the cross, but the apostle Paul did. And though he knew that people regarded the idea of God on a cross as vile and shameful, not only did he preach it, but he gloried in it! He said, "I never want to brag about anything except the cross of our Lord Jesus Christ" (Galatians 6:14 NIRV). This educated, sophisticated, former Jewish rabbi and former Sanhedrin ruler, said that the only thing he found worth bragging about was the cross of Jesus Christ! I find it utterly amazing that God could take the vilest of symbols, one full of humiliation and shame, and turn it into a glorious token of victory.

That God himself would not only visit us, but would allow himself to be viciously nailed to that "emblem of suffering and shame" fills my heart and soul with utter amazement. Only God could do such a thing! Only God could bring glory from shame! He carried on himself the sins of all mankind and died in the most humiliating and shameful way known to man. He was dishonored, disgraced and shamed on the cross.

Brothers and sisters, regardless of what you have done, no matter how shameful and embarrassing it is, "Let us fix our eyes on Jesus, the author and perfecter of our faith, who for the joy set before him endured the cross, scorning its shame." This is what makes Jesus so entirely qualified and able to help us deal with our shame.

In 1 Chronicles 21:13 David said to Gad, "I am in deep distress. Let me fall into the hands of the Lord, for his mercy is very great; but do not let me fall into the hands of men." Men, mere mortals: They can love you, they can care for you, they can listen to you, they can understand, but they are powerless to remove your shame. Only at the feet of Jesus can we safely and confidently lay it all down and say: I am a new creation, a child of God, an heir to the throne; I sit next to the King; I don't care what other people say or what Satan tries to accuse me of, for I fall at the feet of the King of Kings and the Lord of Lords and I bow down to him, and he says to me, "Get up, for I have removed your sin and taken away your shame!"

Coming from a life of homosexuality, many of us have done or thought some incredibly shameful things. As a follower of Jesus you do not have to live in defeat, darkness or secrecy. Come to God. He can handle your sin and shame. It's not too difficult for him. He is not embarrassed or ashamed of you, no matter what you have done or thought. He only longs to love you. He offers freedom from our shame when we listen to who he says we are, rather than what the accuser is trying to sell us.

Quiet Time #5

Flies in the Ointment

I don't appreciate the pharmacist behind the counter at my local drugstore like I need to. I don't think of him unless I need a prescription filled, then all of a sudden he's necessary.

It is a very old and honored profession. Historians tell us that there were pharmacists dating all the way back to the time of Moses. They had no drugstores back then, but there was a man whom every community had who carried the responsibility of making perfumes and medicine for that district. It was considered a very exact science. This person was also considered one of the most respected in society, and his services were continually in demand.

Certainly medicine has undergone significant changes in the last 4,000 years, but many of the foundational elements of this profession have remained the same, for instance, the need for sanitary conscious-ness: Druggists go out of their way by painting their prescription depart-ments all snowy white. Their flasks, funnels and other paraphernalia are always glistening.

Solomon capitalizes on this fact in Ecclesiastes 10:1: "As dead flies give perfume a bad smell, so a little folly outweighs wisdom and honor." Solomon's illustration is that if a conscientious druggist were to have just dispensed a jar of the purest ointment, but then unexpectedly a fly nosedived headlong into the precious compound, then the pharma-cist's salve would have been utterly contaminated and would (by virtue of the contamination) have been ruined, all because of a little fly.

And so the spiritual application for our study: A little sin can ruin your reputation and take away your ability to help others, and in effect, render you useless.

I hate flies. I can't stand it when a fly lands in my food when I am eating or on my nose when I'm trying to sleep. I purchased a drink once with a dead fly in it. Needless to say, I didn't finish the drink. Something can be pure, good and enjoyable, until a little fly pops in, and then all of a sudden it's contaminated and no longer any good.

Solomon's point then is this: Unrepented-of sin is like a dead fly that has gotten into the ointment of our lives, contaminating us. Before we became disciples, we had a lot of flies in our lives, a lot of things that contaminated us. But then Jesus, the ultimate pharmacist, entered our lives and we became clean, pure, righteous and forgiven. We became a pure and precious ointment.

How have you done at keeping the dead flies out of your life? Remember, it only takes one little fly to ruin the whole ointment! In other words, brothers and sisters, there is no such thing as a small sin. We can so easily think to ourselves, "Oh, it's only a little thing; don't exaggerate. A little lie, a little shoplifting, a few little second and third looks, a little hatred, a little porn on the Internet, a little fantasy." How about a little murder?

Matthew 12:35 says: "The good man brings good things out of the good stored up in him, and the evil man brings evil things out of the evil stored up in him." There are many of us who have left the life of homosexuality years ago. We have experienced much victory, and we really don't live the lives we used to live. Yet I want to warn you. You do not need to be enslaved in some gross immoral sin to be contaminated.

To help prove my point, I offer you the story of Naaman as found in 2 Kings 5. The chapter starts by telling us:

> Now Naaman was commander of the army of the king of Aram. He was a great man in the sight of his master and highly regarded, because through him the LORD had given victory to Aram. He was a valiant soldier, but he had leprosy.

Naaman's credentials were incredibly impressive: the commander of the army, a "great man," "highly regarded" and a "valiant soldier"; but he had leprosy. In verse 11 we are told that the leprosy that Naaman had was only a "spot." He body was not covered with this disease; it was only a spot. Now granted, any kind of leprosy obviously is not good, but it's a point that should be noted. You see, even though Naaman was great and highly regarded and valiant, one "spot" of leprosy was enough to endanger his life and take away from all of his amazing qualities.

Likewise it is with us. You may have many tremendous qualities; you may be a loving and compassionate person, have incredible pubic speaking skills, be a leader in your church, be known as a servant, and the list could go on and on. You may carry with you a title like evangelist, church leader, elder or deacon. But just a little unrepented-of sin, something not dealt with, a sin that you hang on to and refuse to take seriously, will damage and hurt you to the point of rendering you ineffective. It is like a dirty little fly that has flown into the pure ointment of your life, rendering you useless.

Brothers and sisters, all sin is serious, all sin needs to be repented of. Let us be reminded of what we are told in 1 Peter 2:11: "Dear friends, I urge you, as aliens and strangers in the world, to abstain from sinful desires, which war against your soul." No matter how far along you are in your journey, regardless of how much "success" you have been blessed with, the devil is warring against you in some area. Please stop and consider your life. Have a time of honest reflection, and get the flies out of the pure ointment that Jesus died for.

Quiet Time #6

An Unfinished Life

It's always interesting to see what the rich and famous did before they became, well, rich and famous. Almost everyone in show business, regardless of who they are today, started off in humble beginnings.

Tom Cruise grew up in a nomadic home, and by the time he was fourteen years old had been in fifteen different schools; he was extremely shy and had few friends. He suffered greatly with dyslexia and because of this problem, school became so difficult that by eleventh grade he was a high-school dropout. But that's not the end of the story; as we all know, Tom Cruise's life was unfinished. Today he is arguably the biggest and most powerful name in the entertainment industry, commanding $25 million dollars a movie.

Eileen Regina Edwards was born in 1965 and grew up in Timmons, Ontario, Canada. The family grew up in relative poverty. Sometimes they would join the local native reservation to hunt for food. Eileen would often take bread with mustard on it to school just to make it appear that she had a lunch, terrified that the authorities would find out and take her away from her family. But throughout all of this, Eileen's mother was determined to nurture her daughter's obvious singing talent. When she was just eight years old, she was performing in front of audiences. From the age of ten, Eileen was writing her own songs and dreaming of a better life. When she was in her teens, she had a job at McDonald's after school.

Then, when she was twenty-one years old and working in Toronto as a secretary, she got the call that would change her life forever. It was the terrible news that her parents had been killed in a car accident. Both of her brothers were also in the vehicle and survived. This turned young Eileen's life upside down. It was now up to Eileen to raise her brothers and sisters and work part-time jobs to see the family through. Those were difficult times for Eileen, but her life was an unfinished one. Eileen is known to the world today as Shania Twain. Her first album, *Come On Over*, is the biggest-selling country album of all time, by any artist, male or female! It is now tied as the fifth-best-selling release, following The Eagles, Michael Jackson, Led Zeppelin and Fleetwood Mac.

Mary J. Blige was a hairdresser in Yonkers, NY.

Luther Vandross worked at a returns desk at a department store.

Eddie Murphy worked in a shoe store.

Chris Rock worked as a busboy in a restaurant, a mental health orderly and also unloaded trucks for the New York Daily News.

Wesley Snipes parked cars at a parking lot.

Whoopi Goldberg worked as a bricklayer and then a funeral-home makeup artist.

Chris Tucker cleaned bathrooms and swept floors for a fast-food restaurant.

Keanu Reeves worked as a janitor.

Rod Stewart worked in a cemetery as a grave digger (that's kind of creepy, isn't it?).

These stories stand out to us because we can see that at this early stage, they were unfinished lives. The Bible is loaded with stories like this about people whose lives were thought to be done but in the hands of Jesus were unfinished lives. The story in John chapter 8 of the woman caught in the act of adultery is one of my favorite, if not my favorite, stories in the entire Bible because it talks of how God looks at us: as unfinished lives.

This story to me is beautiful because it shows how God thinks of each of us: In spite of mistakes and misdeeds, in spite of the severity of our sins, in God's eyes, we are unfinished lives.

As the accusers slowly drifted away and the woman was left alone with Jesus, the beauty of God shone through, because it is here that this woman's life was just beginning, for she was an unfinished life. "Jesus straightened up and asked her, 'Woman, where are they? Has no one condemned you?' 'No one, sir,' she said. 'Then neither do I condemn you,'

Jesus declared. 'Go now and leave your life of sin.'"

This passage shows us two things about the attitude with which people will treat you, compared to how God will treat you. The scribes and Pharisees conceived their function as legal and religious authorities as giving them the right to stand over others like grim reapers, to watch for every mistake, and then to descend on them with unforgiving punishment. They never dreamed that it might lay upon them the obligation to actually help the poor woman.

Welcome to today. There are still those who regard their job as giving them the right to condemn and the duty to punish, and sadly, more often than not, in religious circles. But Jesus shows that true authority, authority from God, is founded on sympathy and mercy. These religious leaders were not looking on this woman as a person. They were looking on her only as a thing, an instrument whereby they could formulate a charge against Jesus. It is extremely unlikely that the scribes and the Pharisees even knew this woman's name. To them she was nothing but a case of shameless adultery, which could now be used as an instrument to suit their purposes. To them, she had no name, no personality, no feelings, no life; she was simply a pawn in the game whereby they sought to destroy Jesus.

But Jesus steps in and shows us that it is always wrong to regard people as things; it is always wrong to regard people as cases, yet this is exactly how we are often treated in our society today when we are in trouble. Man uses authority to order people to change; God uses his authority to love men into goodness; to God no person ever becomes a thing. To God, every person, regardless of their guilt, is a soul capable of moving beyond their failings and a heart, which if given the chance to start over again, can do better.

Don't we all love starting over? Isn't that why birthdays and new years are always so specially marked? They give us all a chance to start over. This is why I became a Christian, and why I stay one today. God, in his infinite mercy, sees not who I was, but who I can be; he continually gives me the opportunity to start over, to begin again.

It is easy to draw the wrong lesson altogether and to gain the impression that Jesus forgave lightly and easily, as if the sin that this woman committed did not matter. Jesus didn't say: "Your sins are forgiven, go and do as you wish and take advantage of my mercy." He said: "I am not going to pass a final judgment now; go and prove that you can do better. You have sinned; go and sin no more."[3]

It is as if he is saying to the woman: "I know you have made a mess of things; I know your life is a train wreck, but life is not finished yet; I am giving you another chance, the chance to redeem yourself." Jesus was always intensely interested, not only in what a person had been, but also in what a person could be. He did not say that what they had done did not matter, but he was sure that every man and woman has a future as well as a past.

The basic difference between Jesus and the scribes was that they wished to condemn; he wished to forgive. But Jesus' attitude also involved challenge: he confronted this woman with the challenge of the sinless life. He did not say: "It's all right; don't worry; just go on as you are doing." He said: "It's all wrong; go out and fight; change your life from top to bottom; go, and sin no more." Jesus confronts the bad life with the challenge of the good.

The amazing, heart-uplifting thing about Jesus was his belief in men and women. He believed that with his help people could change. God's method is not to blast us with the knowledge—which we already possess—that we are sinners, but to inspire us with the unbelievable discovery that we have tremendous potential to be different.[4]

In this story, Jesus also gives each one of us a warning: We are all face to face with the eternal choice. Jesus confronted the woman with a choice that day—either to go back to her old ways or to reach out to the new way with him.

This story is unfinished, for every life is unfinished until it stands before God. All of our lives are "unfinished lives." Who we were and what mistakes we made do not matter to God. What we do today and what we plan to do with the rest of our days—that is what really concerns him. I put before you that left to our own accord, without God, there is not much hope. But it all depends on whose hands our lives are in: our own, or God's.

A basketball in my hands is worth about $19.
A basketball in Shaq's hands is worth about $33 million.
It depends on whose hands it's in.

A baseball in my hands is worth about $6.
A baseball in Roy Halladay's hands is worth $19 million.
It depends on whose hands it's in.

A tennis racket is useless in my hands.
A tennis racket in Venus Williams's hands is championship-winning at Wimbledon.
It depends on whose hands it's in.

A golf club in my hands, is, well, dangerous.
A golf club in the hands of Tiger Woods is history in the making.
It all depends on whose hands it's in.

Two fish and five loaves of bread in my hands is a couple of fish sandwiches.
Two fish and five loaves of bread in God's hands will feed thousands.
It depends on whose hands it's in.[5]

My concerns, worries, fears, hopes and dreams, my family, my relationships, my future: In my hands alone, all of these things are unprotected, bare and exposed, almost destined for defeat, but given over to the hands of a loving, caring and protective Father and God they are safe, secure, on the road to healing and full of hope and promise. It all depends on whose hands they're in.

So it does not matter how messy your life has been. You're in good company, for some of the greatest Bible heroes and heroines had dysfunctional and messy lives. God still used them to do great things, because our God is a God who believes we are capable of doing better.

—Guy Hammond

Chapter Eight Endnotes

1. William Barclay, *The Gospel of John*, 2nd ed., vol. 2 (Edinburgh, Scotland: St. Andrew Press, 1958), 1–3.

2. Ibid.

3. Ibid.

4. Ibid.

5. Adapted from the poem "It Depends On Whose Hands It's In" by Paul Ciniraj.

www.ipibooks.com